Protestant Reformation

Returning to the Word of God

C. P. Hallihan

Trinitarian Bible Society
LONDON, ENGLAND

The Protestant Reformation: *Returning to the Word of God*

Product Code: A128

ISBN 978 1 86228 066 3

TBS

Trinitarian Bible Society

William Tyndale House, 29 Deer Park Road

London SW19 3NN, England

Registered Charity Number: 233082 (England) SC038379 (Scotland)

10M/06/17

Contents:

The Protestant Reformation

Returning to the Word of God

C. P. Hallihan

The Reformation of the sixteenth century is, next to the introduction of Christianity, the greatest event in history. It marks the end of the Middle Ages and the beginning of modern times. Starting from religion, it gave, directly or indirectly, a mighty impulse to every forward movement, and made Protestantism the chief propelling force in the history of modern civilisation.[1]

PHILIP SCHAFF, *History of the Christian Church*

The issues of the Reformation are set out in the unique illustration *Effigies praecipuorum illustrium atque praestantium aliquot theologorum* by the engraver Hans Schwyzer about 1650. Dominating the table in the centre we have the light of the Gospel. On the left sit the leading Protestant reformers (Luther, Zwingli, Calvin, Melanchthon, Bugenhagen and Oecolampadius). Seated opposite are representatives of the Church of Rome. Standing around the table is a crowd of the Reformation's great and good, some more easily recognisable than others: Bullinger (second from left), Knox (sixth from left) and Tyndale (first on the right).

1: A Prologue

The year 2017, marking five hundred years since what many classify as the beginning of the Protestant Reformation, can be viewed from a number of aspects: historical shifts, theological changes, intellectual advances. But our primary interest in this article will be the Bible. During the Reformation,

> The Bible ceased to be a foreign book in a foreign tongue, and became naturalized, and hence far more clear and dear to the common people. Hereafter the Reformation depended no longer on the works of the Reformers, but on the book of God, which everybody could read for himself as his daily guide in spiritual life. This inestimable blessing of an open Bible for all, without the permission or intervention of pope and priest, marks an immense advance in church history, and can never be lost.[2]

Thus we will endeavour to set the history of those times and events in connection with the written Word of God, the Bible: its interaction and impact with events, then as well as before and after.

The 'official' beginning

To erect some 'triumphal arch' of the period 1517 to 2017 would be a great mistake. Regardless of how we define the Protestant 'Reformation', we can be sure it did not begin in 1517, and one sincerely hopes that it is not to end in 2017 (except for the return of the Lord Jesus Christ).

Military pilots learn to avoid the dangers of target fixation—where they are so fixated on the objective that they lose all sense of their surroundings and fly into it—and we assert that '1517 fixation' is not the way to fully understand the Reformation. As good pilots of history, we must consult our navigation aids and maps: theological, historical and geographical,[3] looking behind and all around to see where we are going.

The Bible, the Word of God written, is by Divine purpose under the ministry of the Holy Spirit not only the instrument of redemption, but also of reform. This Word of God is truly the

revelation of Almighty God, and the Gospel of the Lord Jesus Christ is the power of God unto salvation (Romans 1.16).

Both Old and New Testaments show the Scriptures as an instrument of reform unto the people of God. Consider the finding of the book of the law in Josiah's day (2 Kings 22–23), and the words from the risen Christ and King to the seven churches of Revelation 2–3. Neither of those striking Bible summons to reform effected a once-for-all recovery amongst God's people. Nor did the Reformation, even though the first of the Ninety-five Theses reads, 'Our Lord and Master Jesus Christ in saying: "Repent ye", etc., intended that the whole life of believers should be penitence'. Luther had well understood the sense of the seven letters to the churches of Revelation as 'Remember, Repent, and Do!' Over so many zealous conflicts we should hear the voice of Jesus declaring, 'Ye do err, not knowing the scriptures, nor the power of God' (Matthew 22.29).

---

1. Philip Schaff, *History of the Christian Church (the Complete Eight Volumes in One)*, Kindle edition.

2. Ibid.

3. Where things happen is almost as important for insight as when. Useful desk companion of the past months has been Tim Dowley's *Atlas of the European Reformations* [note the use of the plural 'reformations' in the title] (Oxford, England: Lion Books, 2015), and the much wider ranging *Atlas of the Renaissance* (several authors; London, England: Cassell Illustrated, 1993).

The Peasant Wedding Feast ***by Pieter Bruegel the Elder, 1567. The Bruegels are renowned for paintings that provide us with a window on ordinary, everyday life in the sixteenth century and the world of the Reformation period.***

2: Before 1517

A: A very short geographical fix

Forget all knowledge of modern Europe, other than an outline map. The Italian peninsula, for example, was ruled by competing cities—Florence, Genoa, Naples, Milan, Venice and so on—whose extent of territory varied from year to year with military and political success or defeat. The Papal States were a swathe running north-east from Rome to Ferrara.

Naples and Sicily were under the influence of Spain, and in the German states of the Habsburgs things were even more complex. France had a name, but no cohesion outside the major towns and connecting routes by river and road, and a scarcely populated wilderness in between.

Bohemia/Hungary reached the Adriatic Coast, and Poland/Lithuania struggled with each other for supremacy in a domain which stretched at times from the Baltic to the Black Sea. England, Scotland, Wales, Ireland: these western islands raised their heads on occasion. The far western continents had only just been discovered. Latin was the lingua franca of church and education. The Bible was in Latin and unobtainable by those outside church hierarchy. And even if the common man could lay his hands on a copy he would be unable to read it.

B: Precursors and their Bibles; then came printing

The Precursors

The catacombs of Rome provided for persecuted Christians a well-hidden venue to meet in secret.

There were many precursors to the 1517 Reformation. In our *Quarterly Record* we have featured several of these in recent years: the Waldensians, Wycliffe, Hus and the Hussites for example. But ever since the 'church of the catacombs' had been morphed into the 'church of the capitol' in the Latin West,[4] there were individuals, congregations and movements oppressed by the empty failures of medieval Christianity and suppressed by Rome. They often saw the need for submission solely to the rule of God's Word, and following from that the need for accessible Scriptures (in terms of language, number, and right of use), and often paid for this understanding with their blood.

Here I must confess to an inadequacy; I know too little about the Eastern churches. Greek, Russian, Armenian and others, as well as the North African congregations. It is too easy and unhelpful simply to dismiss them all as heretical. Some were mission-minded, and the later Protestant missionaries found long-established Armenian congregations and preachers in surprising and well-scattered places east of the Mediterranean; there were also congregations attributing their origin to the labours of the Apostle Thomas heading towards India. None of these ever seemed to be persecution- or power-play minded, and thus fell out of sight to those in the West that were. Dean Stanley in his *Lectures on the History of the Eastern Church*[5] quotes a Greek bishop as saying 'let foreigners[6] bring us light and we will thank them for it. But we beg of them not to bring fire to burn our house about our ears'.

The Eastern churches regarded the growing power and influence of the Bishop of Rome with grave suspicion and uneasiness. Those problems culminated in the Great Schism, generally dated 1054, in which East and West took their separate paths. Could the Eastern churches be considered proto-Protestants? Probably not: the

The motto of the Waldensians: 'The light shines in the darkness'

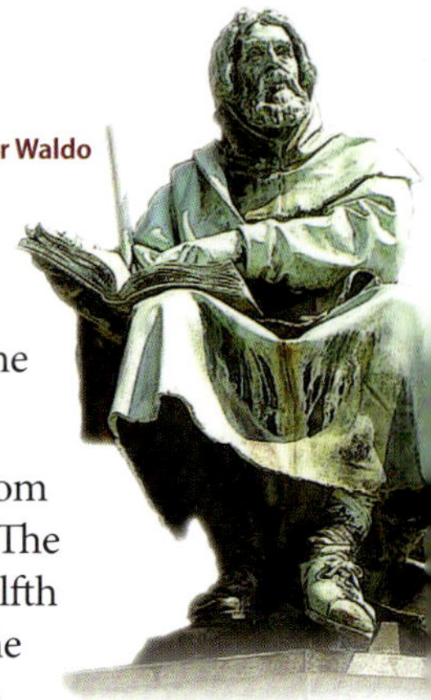

Peter Waldo

differences between East and West were theological as well as cultural.

The East did not stand opposed to the activities of the Western church nor did they want thorough reformation as Wycliffe and the Hussites did.

But then neither did the Waldensians, whom some class as amongst the pre-reformers. The followers of Peter Waldo from the late twelfth century simply went their own spiritual way, with Christ and the Scriptures as their guide, embracing and suffering for the Truth. With both Waldensians and Wycliffites however, their faith, hope and perseverance were sustained by their Bible—translated, as it was, into their own languages from the Latin—and they had a determination to have, and to share widely, the Book in their vernacular.

There were also very different precursors: those who resisted, exposed and denounced the power, errors and ungodliness of the Roman Catholic Church but doing so without the truth of the Gospel. Despite their lack of spiritual understanding, these too were contributors under God to the breaking up of the monolithic structures of the medieval church. Take as an example Girolamo Savonarola, 1452–1498, who preached in Florence on the sinfulness and apostasy of the time. For a while he was very popular but his gospel, often based on visions, was law, to be enacted through repression. This rigour, coupled with claims to the gift of prophecy, brought the charge of heresy. Found guilty, he and two disciples were hanged and

Girolamo Savonarola and his execution in Florence in 1498

burned on 23 May 1498, still professing their adherence to the church, though not to Christ or the Gospel.

Too often for convenience we still hold to a 1517 date for the beginning of the Reformation. But only very recently I stumbled upon this statement in *The Cambridge Companion to Reformation Theology*:[7]

> If there is one thing that can be called a genuine breakthrough in the last half-century of Reformation studies, it would be the 'discovery' that the Reformation had a background.

Exactly. And for us that background reveals the sovereign will, purpose and power of Almighty God, accomplishing all things from Adam's fall to the new earth and heaven, and with grace prevailing.

Early Vernacular Bibles

Luther's Ninety-five Theses may mark the beginning, but the Reformation is seen more specifically in the reclaiming of the New Testament through renewed interest in Greek manuscripts and study. It was followed by faithful exposition and translation into the vernacular tongues, both accompanied by unmistakable testimonies of saving faith in Christ Jesus. This was reformation begun.

Surprisingly enough, the Latin is among the very earliest vernacular translations, the New Testament being translated from the Greek of the Apostles into the common or vulgar tongue of the residual Roman Empire. (Discussing this with an Orthodox clergyman some years ago he chaffed me about the matter—'What is all this fuss about the Erasmus 1516 Greek New Testament? We had it all along'.) How Jerome's AD 405 revision of the Latin Bible came to dominate in the West is another story, but part of the fruit of this was that most of the vernacular work in the West from 405 to 1516 was based on Latin and not on Greek and Hebrew.

On this Latin basis the Bible had been translated into a dozen languages by AD 500, including the Gothic transcription by Ulfilas in the third century. In 865 Cyril and Methodius produced a Slavic Bible; by 995 Anglo-Saxon translations were being produced. Remote Iceland had

Jerome in his study
by Antonio da Fabriano, 1451

The Ostomir Gospels, Slavonic New Testament dating back to 1057

translations and paraphrases of Bible portions in manuscript form, the *Stjórn*, through the thirteenth and fourteenth centuries. Peter Waldo's own translation from Latin into a form of their Romaunt was presented to the Pope in 1179, and Catalan manuscripts of the Waldensian version are said to have been extant in the thirteenth century.

Perhaps it was in the light particularly of the resulting Waldensian 'heresy' that it was decreed in 1229 that only a priest could own a Bible. Ignoring this, in 1382 John Wycliffe produced his magnificent English translation, owned of God to the saving of souls and furnishing his Lollard preachers with a plain, firm foundation for the preaching of 'this gospel of the kingdom'.[8] Then there were the early Czech Bibles of the Hussites, gladly following Wycliffe's lead: Scriptures that nearly resulted even then in reformation.

All this Bible work was handwritten. What could be done literally to spread the Word widely when each copy had to be so laboriously produced, often in secret and under cover? Who can deny that God's hand was in the work of Gutenberg!

Printing

Johann Gutenberg (1400?–1468) of Mainz, Germany was a silversmith by profession and familiar with the process of duplicating metalwork from a cast or 'type' of an original. Around 1430–1440 he developed the use of movable, interchangeable, reusable letter-type for printing copies of documents.

Movable metal type was used in the printing industry right up until the late twentieth century, when it was largely replaced by digital technology.

His first printings were reputedly copies of the indulgence statements which were being sold by the Roman Catholic Church to raise funds for building projects in exchange for reduction of temporal punishment for sins—documents which would lead Luther sixty years later to pen his Ninety-five Theses. Gutenberg built a wooden press similar to those used for wine or

Johann Gutenberg

cheese making, and produced a printing ink of his own concocting: an oily, varnish-like ink made of soot, turpentine and walnut oil.

Gutenberg's masterpiece, of course, was the Latin Bible printed in 1453–1454; there were 180 copies made, each of 1,282 pages and having 42 lines in two columns. (Bible collectors' eyes grow misty at these words!) The Bibles were completed by hand-colouring the main capitals.

The Gutenberg Bible

This new print-shop business was backed financially by a man called Fust (or Faust). The time came for Fust to call in his money—some claim not quite scrupulously. After a lawsuit Fust took possession of the press in default of payment, leading to aimless controversies over the years as to who actually printed the 1453 Bible. Erasmus said it was Fust, but today this first printed Bible is known widely as the Gutenberg Bible.

The early print process, once the type had been set up, aimed to produce around six pages of a book per day. If that doesn't sound many in comparison to those produced by a skilled and well-practiced scribe, remember that each day the press would print multiple identical copies of each page. With a typeset page, there were soon figures of twenty-five pages per hour on this basis. Improving the setting-up speed became a

An early printing press typical of the period

priority, and mass production of books had begun. Before 1500 a single press could produce 3,600 book pages in a working day, so that the works of Erasmus and Luther were sold by hundreds of thousands in their own lifetimes.

This art of printing by movable type had been almost a trade secret in Mainz until after 1462, when the city was plundered during an argument between two feuding bishops. After that, printing presses proliferated. They appeared in Rome in 1467, Venice in 1469, Paris in 1470, Cracow in 1474, Westminster (London) in 1476, and on across Europe, numbering about 250 by the early 1500s. The production of 27,000 print editions by that time was impressive; but on the other hand only one per cent of Europe's population owned any book! For information and communication, the pulpit and the marketplace were still more useful than the written word.

Printed vernacular Bibles were to change all of this as people were becoming eager to read for themselves the truths of religion. The Bible in your own language was, and is, the perfect book to learn the truth of life, death and eternity. One literate friend or family member could read aloud the Scriptures in your hearing and in your own language, and so you also could begin to learn to read. Outside the scholarly/clerical world (essentially the same thing in Europe at that time) such acquisition of literacy had not often happened, and then it would almost certainly be in Latin. Literacy and literature were the catalysts for and results of what would in time be called the Renaissance.

---

4. The church which had endured underground in Rome now had pomp, circumstance and power in Rome: the embryonic papacy had begun.

5. A. P. Stanley, *Lectures on the History of the Eastern Church*, quoted in Joseph Dent, *Everyman's Library* (London, England: J. M. Dent and Sons, Ltd, 1924), p. 93.

6. I think he means other kinds of Christians.

7. David V. N. Bagchi and David C. Steinmetz, *The Cambridge Companion to Reformation Theology* (Cambridge, England: Cambridge University Press, 2004), p. 5.

8. Cf. Matthew 24.14.

3: The Renaissance

The Renaissance is defined as 'The revival of arts and letters under the influence of classical models, which began in Italy in the fourteenth century'.[9] The word is directly from French, meaning rebirth, and a timeline in the *Atlas of the Renaissance* runs from 1302 to 1610.[10] As a movement of general concern with style and taste it lingered well into the nineteenth century.

More specifically, for an understanding of the Reformation the Renaissance relates to the recovery of copies of ancient texts and manuscripts in Greek, Latin and, later, Arabic, along with old translations between those languages. The impact of this on scholars for philosophy, religion, design and general sense of historical reconnection, was profound.

From the Apostles' time, through Jerome's era and after, even as far as Bede in 735, New Testament study and commentary had usually been based on Greek Scriptures. The Church Fathers, in their search for a better understanding of their Greek New Testament, certainly noted variations encountered between readings in the Greek manuscripts and the Latin texts that they used. Their Latin Testament they recognised quite rightly as a translation, and not an original.

Bede

However from Bede's time for some seven hundred years, use or even awareness of Greek diminished almost to vanishing point in the West, and its study was viewed as heretical and schismatic. Roger Bacon (1220–1292) was among the earliest to renew the suggestion, even insistence, that Bible scholars really must learn Greek and Hebrew, and on this only should they base their expositions, commentaries and accurate Biblical texts.[11]

Roger Bacon

Where had this store of ancient and Biblical literature been for the years preceding the Renaissance, and why did it seem to reappear all at once? The Holy Roman Empire in the West officially fell in 1250,[12] but since 406 when the Barbarians had pierced the frontiers, crossing the frozen Rhine, it had been but a poor, lingering shadow of an empire. In 410 the Goths sacked Rome, and then the Vandals attacked in 455. In religion these

Invasion of the Barbarians by Ulpiano Checa y Sanz, 1887

Goths and Vandals were, if anything, Arians (denying the eternity of God the Son). The last nominal Western emperor was deposed in 476.

All of this had left Constantinople well established as sole heir of Imperial Rome, and encouraged the long-standing trend for Greek material, sacred and profane, to go east to Byzantium. Ancient Latin literature also accumulated there. In general there were very few ordinary dealings between Constantinople and Rome.

John Bessarion

However, John Bessarion (1403–1472), born in Trebizond (now Trabzon, Turkey), was educated at Constantinople and then became a monk. In 1437 the Byzantine Emperor John VIII made him archbishop of Nicaea. They two journeyed to Italy seeking some union between the Byzantine and Western churches, and help in the growing struggle against the Turks, now seriously threatening Constantinople. In 1439, in Rome, Pope Eugenius IV made Bessarion a cardinal and he settled there in Italy.

On the large scale, it was all too little too late. The Ottoman Turks besieged and captured Constantinople in 1453, 'ending the Byzantine Empire and the Middle Ages'[13] (how delightfully succinct!). This Turkish conqueror was Mehmet II, the Grand Turk.[14] It was the most terrifying thing that had happened throughout Christendom, outranking even the loss of Jerusalem to Saladin (October 1187). Jerusalem's fall had posed no direct threat to Europe but now such a menace hung over the West as Mehmet with his armies attacked, with marked success, much of southern

John Hunyadi

Europe.[15] Europe then was indebted to the Hungarian John Hunyadi for heroic resistance to the very walls of Buda and Vienna. Nevertheless, Muslim influence in the Balkans—the old Roman Province of Dalmatia—had begun.

For our concerns, this huge derangement did, in God's purpose, displace Greek, Hebrew and classical scholars, with their manuscripts, scholarship and philosophy, mostly toward north Italy. These texts and the linguistic skills needed to access them, along with translations to and from Arabic, escaped to the West. Bessarion in particular spread the knowledge of Greek language and learning. He formed schools of Greek and gathered a library with a large collection of Greek manuscripts, later donated to the Senate of Venice. John Bessarion was given the ceremonial position of Latin (Roman Catholic) patriarch of Constantinople in 1463 and died in November 1472.

***The entry of Mehmet II into Constantinople* by Benjamin Constant, 1876**

In Italy and throughout Europe the impact of this increase in knowledge was seen in numerous ways as scholars gained access to clearer sources of ancient culture. Rediscovery of the Latin writings of Lucretius (99–55 BC) and the Greek of Epicurus (341–271 BC), among others, irrevocably changed philological and scientific criticism and historical research, but not always for the better as the religious and moral views from pagan antiquity were also now reacquired. This heritage was idolatrous and polytheistic in religion, with amorality prevailing in practice.

We must not ignore the sizeable Trojan Horse of plain pagan heathenism—and this to our continuing confusion five hundred years later. Today's prevailing philosophical satisfaction with self as the chief end of man is directly from the Greek Epicurus via the Latin Lucretius to the Renaissance Man and our Modern Man also. Their creed declares that there is no God, no guilt, no afterlife: thus 'do what you want to do' and every man doing what is right in his own eyes (Judges 21.25). Too many of the great names of the Renaissance subscribed in some degree to this ethos, with titles like Christian Humanism as a fig leaf.

Nonetheless we must be glad of this reconnection with classical learning, literature and manners after 1453, thankful to God for this renewal of linguistic skills and materials relating to the Scripture and its interpretation. From a purely scholarly viewpoint: the uncouth, awkward, unfriendly Latin of scholastic and monastic writers, more likely to confuse than enlighten, was replaced by a classic elegance of style and form, smooth and readable. The much favoured italic script also made its appearance.

More rewarding still was the renewal of the study of the Biblical languages. The Western church was not unaware that the Scriptures were originally written in Greek and Hebrew, but these languages—and the Scriptures in them—had long been lost to the West. The fall of Constantinople in 1453 brought to hand copies of the Greek New Testament Scriptures and men who could read them. Comparing these with the accepted Latin Scriptures confirmed the long-held feeling that the text of the Latin Bible extant in the fifteenth century was, to say the least, unreliable. If the Bible were unreliable, perhaps the teachings supposedly supported by it would also turn out to be equally untrustworthy. Thus, the renewal of the Greek and Hebrew Scriptures brought with it a recognition of truth over falsehood.

Regarding the Greek of the Renaissance and Reformation, few names come to mind before that of Desiderius Erasmus, and few tasks before the all-important collating, editing and printing of the text of a Greek New Testament.

9. *Shorter Oxford English Dictionary*, 2 vols. (Oxford, England: Clarendon Press, 1980).

10. Steven Ozment's book on the times is actually called *The Age of Reform 1250–1550* (London, England: Yale University Press, 1980) and Peter Wallace wrote *The Long European Reformation…1350–1750* (London, England: Palgrave Macmillan, 2004).

11. See for example Edmond Nolan and S. A. Hirsch, *The Greek Grammar of Roger Bacon* (Cambridge, England: Cambridge University Press, 1902), p. xviff.

12. The year of the death of the last Holy Roman Emperor, Frederick II. 'The intense struggle between Frederick and the papacy led to the ruin of the house of Hohenstaufen and severely damaged papal prestige. With his rule the great days of the German empire ended and the rise of states in Italy began' ('Frederick II [Holy Roman Emperor and German King]', *Encyclopedia.com*, www.encyclopedia.com/people/history/german-history-biographies/frederick-ii-holy-roman-empire). Some extend the date to 1806.

13. Gordon Kerr, *Time-Line History of the World* (London, England: Futura Publications, 2007).

14. One extraordinary event of the time concerned one of Mehmet II's two sons, known in the West as Jem Sultan (*Jem Sultan* by John Freely [Glasgow, Scotland: Harper Perennial, 2004] is an interesting read), whose mother tongue was Arabic. He was effectively banished from the Ottoman world by his father and brother, and finished up living at the Papal Palace in Rome. However, rather than serving as the experienced and well-travelled linguist that he was, having had experience in the Balkans with fellow Muslims, and in the complex political atmosphere of France, he was treated as a political pawn.

15. Spain is a different story, not to detain us now.

4: Erasmus

Greek reborn

The most terrifying event for fifteenth-century Europe had been the 1453 fall of Constantinople. The most powerful event of fifteenth century Europe had been the 1450s practical development and use of printing. In His providence our God brought these two events together to significant effect in the life and work of Desiderius Erasmus.[16]

Gerrit Gerritszoon[17] was born the second illegitimate son of a Roman Catholic priest, about 1466. The name Desiderius Erasmus he chose for himself, mingling the Greek and Latin terms of 'pleasing' and 'longing'. The Gerritszoon brothers were put to school in Deventer, but when both parents died their guardians removed them to s-Hertogenbosch under the tutelage of the Brethren of the Common Life.

Erasmus early found the Latin language to be an enduring refuge, which led eventually throughout Europe to his acknowledged and admired mastery of the tongue and its literature. Latin effectually became his 'home', the place where he lived. Only bare rudiments of Greek were acquired at the time.

The guardians sent Erasmus to a monastery of the Augustinians at Steyn, near Gouda, where he encountered the teachings of Lorenzo Valla (1407–1457). That secular, classical humanist was persuaded that medieval scholasticism was a barbarous corruption of the ancient learning in both language and style. Erasmus now considered his monastic guides to be those very barbarians, and his *Antibarbarorum liber* (*Book against the Barbarians*) now began to take shape. The medieval Roman Catholic Church believed secular scholarship to be problematic at best, heretical at worst; Erasmus declared that all true learning was secular. Neither position is tenable; conflict was inevitable.

Albrecht Dürer's engraving of Erasmus

Ordained a priest in April 1492, Erasmus was delivered from the monastery to a post as Latin secretary to the influential Henry of Bergen, bishop of Cambrai. In 1495 this bishop sent him to the University of Paris to study theology. What Erasmus found there—learning by rote from Thomas Aquinas (1225–1274) and Duns Scotus (1266–1308)[18] with no liberty of discussion or allowance of difference—did not suit him at all. He began to take on pupils—to help financially but perhaps also to ease the dull sameness of his studies—and this opened more avenues to him.

From that time, and for the rest of his days, Erasmus became what the monastic world terms 'vagus', a wanderer of no fixed loyalty, obedience or commitment to place, people or vows. One of his pupils, William Blount, 4th Baron Mountjoy, invited Erasmus to England. Erasmus was very glad of the removal to the western islands; in the providence of God it resulted not in the enlargement of his Latin but, rather surprisingly, in the improvement of his Greek through two Englishmen—William Grocyn (1446–1519) and Thomas Linacre (1460–1524), who had learned a living Greek in Italy from a group of Greek speakers who lived together and spoke only Greek.

There was also a rather later Greek scholar from Scotland, **George Wishart (1513–1546)**. Following education in France, then priesthood, Wishart returned to Scotland in 1538, but now was teaching students the New Testament in Greek. The Bishop of Brechin furiously drove him out of the land, and Wishart spent three years in Switzerland. He returned to Scotland, via Cambridge, in 1543, and was executed as a heretic in 1546. This was a compelling example to John Knox, who followed his path to Geneva and back to Scotland.

The touchstone of this Greek school in Italy for forty years and more was Demetrios Chalkokondyles, 1423–1511.[19] He moved to Italy in 1444 and arrived in Rome in 1449 where Cardinal Bessarion (see pages 18 and 19) became his patron. Chalkokondyles lived the rest of his life in Italy as a teacher of Greek and philosophy. An Italian pupil described his lectures at Perugia in 1450 thus:

> A Greek has just arrived, who has begun to teach me with great pains, and I to listen to his precepts with incredible pleasure, because he is Greek, because he is an Athenian, and because he is Demetrius [sic]… Merely seeing him you fancy you are looking on Plato; far more when you hear him speak.[20]

Demetrios Chalkokondyles

In Florence, Chalkokondyles edited Homer for publication. This was subsequently counted as his major accomplishment. But lovers of our Greek New Testament may have a different evaluation, preferring Scriptural truth to classical myth, however engagingly written.

A fascinating morsel from Demetrios's time at Florence is that the German classical scholar Johannes Reuchlin was one of his pupils. Reuchlin was to be a close rival of Erasmus in the Greek New Testament story, and we should lament the fact that Reuchlin, having acquired his Greek from a Greek, had a far superior pronunciation, whereas what subsequently came down to years and years of New Testament Greek study was rather Erasmus's awkward Latinate pronunciation. Demetrios, by the way, also produced the Byzantine *Suda* (Σοῦδα) lexicon in 1499 and a Greek grammar edited in 1546 by Melchior Volmar in Basel.

Johannes Reuchlin

John Colet (1467–1519), who so roundly disabused Erasmus of the value of Aquinas, had followed his English compatriots William Grocyn and Thomas Linacre to Italy. He also found there in such Greek corners of the peninsula Christian teachings of the New Testament: the plain, simple record of the facts of the life of Christ, and a few apostolic letters to the churches, all declaring the Person of the Messiah, Jesus Christ, to be the only and necessary object of faith.[21] This teaching reached Erasmus, and how indebted we are to him for he was, under God, a human instrument by which the Word of God was faithfully translated from the printed Greek texts he compiled into several major European languages.

John Colet

Erasmus and these other men were recipients of the benefits of the fall of Constantinople and of the advent of printing. The Biblical language texts—and the ability to read them—flowed west from the destroyed capital, and European entrepreneurs made the most of the newly-discovered techniques of printing to place those texts into hungry hands.

But what about Hebrew?

We cannot leave the text and printing of the Scriptures without brief reference to the Hebrew Bible, our Old Testament. Jewish printers quickly saw the advantages of the printing press. For synagogue services written scrolls were, and are still, sufficient; but print was soon found useful in providing private copies of the Hebrew Bible. Abraham ben Hayyim dei Tintori printed the first book in Hebrew in 1474 (probably a section of *halacha*—Jewish law), but the first printed portion of the Hebrew Bible was in 1477. That was three hundred copies of the Psalms, with David

Abraham ben Hayyim dei Tintori's printed Scripture portion, 1478 edition, housed at the Medici Laurentian Library, Bologna

Kimchi's commentary on each verse. The first edition of the Pentateuch came in Bologna in 1482, with targumim (Aramaic paraphrases) and Rashi's commentary printed on the page with the text.

The Soncino Press of Gerson ben Moses Soncino, a name still in use in the Hebrew publishing world, was established in Brescia and issued a Pentateuch with the five *megillot* (Song of Solomon, Ruth, Lamentations, Ecclesiastes and Esther) and the *haftarot* (selections of the Prophets for synagogue reading) in January 1492; other portions followed, with a complete Bible in May 1494. This edition is of special interest as it was used by Luther in making his translation into German. Luther's copy is preserved in the Berlin State Library.

Daniel Bomberg of Antwerp printed the first edition of Mikraot Gedolot (the Rabbinic Bible, which includes the Masoretic notes on the Biblical text) in Venice in

1517. The second Bomberg text, of 1525, edited by Jacob ben Chayyim, set enduring standards: this text, more than any other, influenced all later printed Hebrew Bibles. The improved edition—that of Everado van der Hooght in 1705—served as the basis of all the modern editions of the Hebrew text until the Leningrad Codex of 1008 was brought into use in 1937.[22]

While Greek was the language of primary interest to most, very many of the reformers acquired a competence in Hebrew. Tyndale was remarkable in this; his knowledge was so great that many have taken the view that stories of his ability in the language are apocryphal, but to no avail.

---

16. For a more full account, please see *Quarterly Record* no. 615, April to June 2016, pp. 30–41.

17. Many alternatives, in English and German, are offered, but this I stumbled upon in a 2015 history lesson plan for a Dutch school.

18. Aquinas was the unquestioned ruler of theology. Duns Scotus gave us 'dunce' in English; the D-cap in the corner meant you had not memorised your day's rote of Duns Scotus. William Farel (1489–1565) and John Calvin (1509–1564) endured the same 'education' at the same university in their days!

19. Born in Athens his brother, Laonikos Chalkokondyles, was the contemporary author of a chronicle of the fall of Constantinople.

20. Ellwood Patterson Cubberley, *The History of Education* (Charleston, SC, USA: BiblioBazaar, LLC, 2008), 1.264.

21. What will our God do to preserve, recover, and redistribute his own Word, the Bible? As Joseph's bones were returned to the Promised Land (Exodus 13.19), so have the Scriptures been recovered from exile many times, and by unlikely or unexpected agencies—sometimes spanning great numbers of years, of generations. As an incorrigible bookworm I must always celebrate the finding again of a misplaced book by reading it through, again, at once. By how very much greater the joyous consequence of the Scripture of Truth newly recovered (cf. 2 Kings 22.8ff).

22. Much is made by some about this change, but it must be noted that the consonantal text of the Leningrad Codex differs from that of Bomberg and van der Hooght in only eight instances.

5: Up to and after 1517[23]

A: Wittenberg: Martin Luther 1483–1546

Hans and Margaret Luther

A second son was born to Hans and Margaret Luther (or Ludher) on 10 November 1483 in Eisleben, Thuringia.[24] The boy was baptised the next day, St. Martin's day, 11 November, and given the saint's name.[25] At school in Mansfeld, age seven, young Luther studied the trivium of grammar, rhetoric and logic. Age fourteen he moved to the cathedral school in Magdeburg, lodging with the Brethren of the Common Life, and then in 1498 to a parish school in Eisenach. University life began in Erfurt in 1501, with B.A. in 1503 and M.A. in 1505. The same year, anxious distress (*Anfechtung*) as to the state of his soul[26] brought him to the Augustinian Monastery in Erfurt, and possibly the first sight of a Bible. Sent to the University of Wittenberg in 1508, he was awarded the Bible Baccalaureate in 1509, and sent to Rome on Augustinian business in 1510. There the shocks to his perception of the papacy and to the basis of his own salvation are well known.

Luther's birthplace

Returning to Wittenberg, Luther was made Professor for Bible there, and awarded a Doctorate in Theology, swearing to preach and teach the Scripture faithfully. (Little did they know just how faithfully!) He held the post, and upheld the oath, for the rest of his life, even as events in that life changed the world. From 1514 he preached regularly in the Wittenberg town church.

The City of Eisleben, the setting for both Luther's birth in 1483 and death in 1546

Clear indication of his path came with the printed sermons on the penitential Psalms, written not for educated Nurembergers but for 'raw Saxons',[27] published in 1517. That same year excesses in the Roman Catholic Church moved him to draw up ninety-five theses for a proposed 'disputation on the value of indulgences'.[28]

Indulgences were the supposed remission of sins by payment of money to the papacy via paper acquittals and were openly sold in the markets and villages of Europe. Such an indulgence (counted in days: more money paid, more days indulged) was supposed to cut down the time to be spent in purgatory (according to Roman Catholic doctrine, the place of purging sins before one could be accepted into heaven). The pope allegedly could draw upon Christ's merits for the benefit of those who gave money for the benefit of the Roman Church. Thus, the pope claimed to be able to do what Christ's death on the cross through the gift and exercise of faith could not. The rebuttal of this and the reclaiming of the truth of the gospel—the sovereign sufficiency of Christ alone to save—is the heart doctrine of the Reformation.

Luther nails his theses to the Wittenberg church door

Luther's theses, in their original Latin form, were posted on the famous Wittenberg church door and sent to the Archbishop of Mainz in October 1517, but there was to be no disputation. The University of Mainz sent a copy to Rome, and there were demands that Luther be silenced. In the meantime the printing press came into its own as copies of the theses in Latin along with a German translation were printed and circulated in Wittenberg and Nuremberg.

By 1518 Luther's attention was turning to the Scriptures in his native German but also in the Biblical languages. In his Introduction to a 1518 edition of the anonymous fourteenth-century mystical treatise *Theologia Deutsch*[29] he wrote, 'I thank God that I have found and heard my God in the German tongue, as neither I nor they have yet found him in the Latin, Greek or Hebrew tongue'.[30] Bible editions and preaching in the vernacular language, anchored in reliable Biblical language texts, became a keystone of the Reformation, the ground of sola scriptura.[31]

In a 1524 booklet ***Those who give cause for Disturbance*** (in Zurich) Zwingli had listed as problematic:

Merely anti-catholic 'evangelicals'

Libertine 'evangelicals'

Agitators about tithes *(cash-value 'evangelicals'?)*

Anti-paedobaptists

Roman Catholic clergy, from bishops to monks and nuns

Catholic Princes

Philip Melanchthon

Three treatises came from Luther in 1520: an appeal to the German princes to reform the church if no one else would, a discussion of the sacraments, and *On Christian Freedom*. This last was his setting out of the truth of justification by faith, the unique instrument of connection between Christ and the believer: sola fide. This teaching of justification by faith led Luther inevitably to predestination and election, and therefore to fierce controversy with Erasmus. However, Luther's emphatic delight was always now to be in the direct, personal experience of God in Christ in repentance, grace, and justification by faith. The record of his own path to this conviction and assurance has usually moved believers to a sense of loving friendship with him, despite differences in other areas.

By 1520 Luther's standing with the Roman Catholic Church was in disarray, and the next year he was excommunicated. The ban on Luther and his writings fell to the secular authorities, culminating in the Diet of Worms (a legal church convocation held in the city of Worms) later that year. He was declared an outlaw, his writings were classified as heresy and burned, and Luther was forced to flee.

More German Reformation history at this point is not within the remit of this booklet, and Martin Luther died in 1546. But we must mention Philip Melanchthon (Greek form *melas* [μέλας] of his surname Schwartzerd, 'black earth'), 1497–1560. He had been appointed Professor of Greek at Wittenberg in 1516, becoming Luther's fellow worker, supporter, amanuensis and confidant. He composed the Augsburg Confession of 1530, and led the German Reformation after Luther's death until losing the confidence of many Protestants by making concessions to Rome. He also made quite complex theological refinements of Luther's views on law and gospel—admittedly never quite static even for Luther himself—but problematic for some followers of Luther.

Often the word 'protestant' is prefaced to 'reformation', bringing the question 'what is a Protestant?' In 1526, an Imperial Diet[32] held in Speyer, Germany, passed an Edict of Toleration, allowing the assembled princes and magistrates to determine the religious practice of their domain. This gave some elbow room for reformation, but in 1529 another Diet of Speyer revoked the Edict of Toleration. The Roman Catholic Latin mass was to be allowed everywhere, and all groups denying the presence of Christ in the Eucharist or who rejected infant baptism were to be forbidden. This provoked a formal protest from fourteen cities and five territories. Their protest, drafted with Melanchthon's help, held that they were being asked to deny the Lord Jesus Christ and reject his Word. It was presented and ignored, so that the protesters drew up a treaty of mutual support, so becoming known as Protestants.

There is also a sad foretaste of future alignments, for when Zurich wanted to join the protest, the city was refused because Zwingli's theology was not in line with Luther's. The Protestants became divided—Wittenberg or Zurich. So another Diet was convened at Augsburg, at which the cities were to present their statements of faith. Melanchthon drafted and presented the Wittenberg statement—*Confessio Augustana*, the Augsburg Confession. It was not acceptable to the emperor. For safety the Protestant territories formed the Schmalkaldic League, a religious and military association of Protestant cities and countries. Membership was open to Augsburg Confession subscribers, which thus became the defining statement of Lutheran doctrine (modern Lutheranism arguably owes rather more to Melanchthon than Luther). Luther's life, in its anguished path to justification and salvation by grace through faith, is the real Luther.

German postage stamp issued in 1980 celebrating the 450th anniversary of the Augsburg Confession

23. England is sometimes said to have had a 'Long Reformation' from 1500 to 1800. This then is the 'short Reformation' from the Ninety-five Theses to the end of the Council of Trent. The towns used as headings relate as much to the Bible as to Reformation.

24. At that time and for long after, it makes more sense to speak of 'The Germanies' than simply 'Germany'. Small princedoms, bishoprics and palatinates were loosely gathered under some shifting Imperial power.

25. The following year Johann Agricola was born in Eisleben; he was also to be numbered among the Protestant Reformers, friend and then opponent of Luther.

26. During a thunderstorm a lightning bolt hit nearby. Terrified of Divine judgment, Luther called out for help to his favourite saint, promising to become a monk if she would protect him.

27. Erasmus also condemned those who seemed to think that the Scriptures were 'only fit for the perfumed'.

28. As the Theses are properly titled.

29. Luther thought this was written by the German mystic Tauler.

30. Charlotte Methuen, *Luther and Calvin: Religious Revolutionaries* (Oxford, England: Lion Books, 2011), p. 23.

31. 'By Scripture alone' proclaims that Scripture is the only basis for faith and practice. It did not sit well with the Roman view of Scripture plus church tradition, and still does not. But today how many Protestant seminaries and colleges teach Greek and Hebrew at all, even as a minority option?

32. 'An assembly of princes and delegates, the chief national council in several countries in Europe' (Thomas Davidson, *Chambers's Twentieth Century Dictionary*, 1908 edn., en.wikisource.org/wiki/Chambers%27s_Twentieth_Century_Dictionary_1908/Deteriorate_Diptera, accessed 10 November 2016.

6: Luther's Translation of the Bible

The Archbishop of Mainz had in 1486 issued a prohibition of all unauthorised printing of sacred and learned books, and especially Scriptures, in German. He held the German language to be incapable of rendering the profound sense of Greek and Latin works; he was certain that laymen and women could not understand the Bible anyway. A prominent German humanist, Geiler of Kaysersberg, who was sharply critical of the abuses of the Roman Catholic Church, nevertheless also thought it an evil thing to print the Bible in German. Thank God for Luther and his experience of the saving wisdom in the truth of the Bible; he had the prime qualification to be a translator: a Christian, devout, faithful, diligent, learned, spiritually experienced, well exercised in heart.

IN CLYTA BASILEA

DAs neuw Testamēt recht grüntlich teütscht.

Mit gantz gelerten vnd richtigen vorredē/vnd der schwerestē örterē kurtz/aber gůt/auslegung.

Ein gnůgsam Regi/ster/wo man die Epistlen vnd Euangelien des gantzen jars in disem Testa ment finden soll.

Die auslendigen wörtter/auff vnser teütsch gewendet vnd gebessert.

Gedruckt zum dritten mal/durch Adam Petri zů Basel/Anno M. D. xxv.

1523

ADAM PETRI

Title page to Luther's New Testament, 1530 edition

Luther's excommunication resulted in what can be considered an enforced internal exile in Wartburg Castle, imposed for his own safety. It was here in 1522 that he gave to the German people his most important and useful work—the translation of Erasmus's Greek New Testament into German: the first fruits of Erasmus's 1516 Greek Testament. It brought the teaching and example of Christ and the Apostles

Marktkirche, Halle

directly to the mind and heart of newly awakened German people—Luther's 'raw Saxons'—in their common tongue and from the authentic Biblical Greek text rather than a corrupt Latin translation.[33]

The German people embraced this book in church, school and home. The Bible was now not a remote book in a foreign tongue, but in the everyday language: homely, clear and dear to people. Luther insisted that he had listened to the speech of the mother at home, the children in the street, the men and women in the market, the butcher and various tradesmen in their shops. The Luther New Testament, and all editions revised under his own guidance, certainly bears this out.

In the city of Halle there is one of the earliest Protestant church libraries in Germany, the *Marienbibliothek* at the Marktkirche, established in 1552. It was founded in response to a call from Martin Luther to create Protestant schools and libraries: Christian education at all levels of society.

The veracity of the Reformation in Germany and the works of the Reformers could now easily be verified and confirmed in the Scripture. Anyone could read for himself, to friends and family, needing neither the permission from nor suffering the intervention of priests. The New Testament was followed by Genesis to Song of Solomon in 1523–1524 and Prophets in 1532, all from Hebrew sources. The

The Wartburg Castle

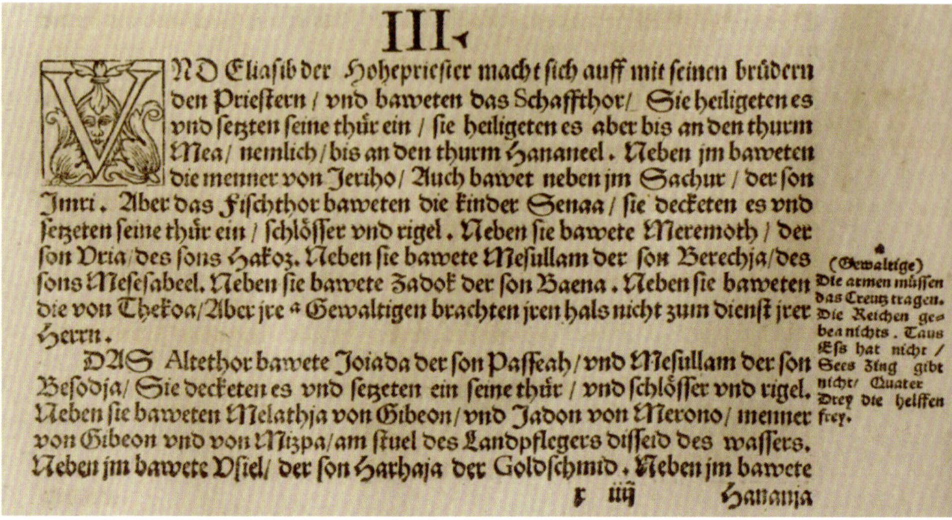

III.

VND Eliasib der Hohepriester macht sich auff mit seinen brüdern
den Priestern / vnd baweten das Schaffthor / Sie heiligeten es
vnd setzten seine thür ein / sie heiligeten es aber bis an den thurm
Mea / nemlich / bis an den thurm Hananeel. Neben jm baweten
die menner von Jericho / Auch bawet neben jm Sachur / der son
Imri. Aber das Fischthor baweten die kinder Senaa / sie deckten es vnd
setzeten seine thür ein / schlösser vnd rigel. Neben sie bawete Meremoth / der
son Vria / des sons Hakoz. Neben sie bawete Mesullam der son Berechja / des
sons Mesesabeel. Neben sie bawete Zadok der son Baena. Neben sie baweten
die von Thekoa / Aber jre a Gewaltigen brachten jren hals nicht zum dienst jrer
Herrn.

DAS Altethor bawete Joiada der son Passeah / vnd Mesullam der son
Besodja / Sie deckten es vnd setzeten ein seine thür / vnd schlösser vnd rigel.
Neben sie baweten Melathja von Gibeon / vnd Jadon von Merono / menner
von Gibeon vnd von Mizpa / am stuel des Landpflegers disseid des wassers.
Neben jm bawete Vsiel / der son Harhaja der Goldschmid. Neben jm bawete

x iiij Hanaja

a (Gewaltige) Die armen müssen das Creutz tragen. Die Reichen gebe nichts. Taus Es ist hat nicht / Sees Zing gibt nicht / Quater Drey die helffen frey.

A sample from Nehemiah 3 in Luther's Bible

whole Bible—*Biblia, das ist: die gantze Heilige Schrifft Deudsch*—was published in 1534. Luther, being as great a Latinist as Erasmus, would certainly have had an eye on the Vulgate too; but his primary sources were the Biblical language texts.

Despite prohibitions and persecutions, soon this Bible appeared in sixteen or seventeen editions, and over fifty reprints—not all of them authorised—as the people clamoured for the Word of God in their language. Luther complained of the many errors in such irregular and irresponsible editions, and yet never ceased to amend his translation. He corrected errors, improved uncouth and confused orthography (too Gothic), fixed the grammar, and cleared the vocabulary of obscure and ignoble words. Luther himself prepared five editions of his whole Bible, the last in 1545—a year before his death.

This last became the proper basis of all standard editions of Luther's Bible: a German *textus receptus* in its own right. The slogan 'what was not done by Luther's hand is not the Luther Bible' became a plumb line held up to all later editions. However, verse divisions appeared first in a Heidelberg reprint of 1568, and 1 John 5.7 (which was absent from Erasmus's 1516 Greek due to limited manuscript access but added in his third edition) was first included by a Frankfurt publisher of 1574. Elector August of Saxony tried to control the text in the interest of strict Lutheran orthodoxy, ordering a standard edition in 1581, but this was disregarded outside of Saxony.

Cochlaeus, who early on was briefly interested in Luther's ministry but later become a fierce champion of Romanism, had this to say:

> Luther's New Testament had been reproduced by the printers to an amazing degree, so that even shoemakers and women and every kind of unlearned person, whoever of them were Lutherans and had somehow learned German letters, read it most eagerly as the font of all truth. And by reading and rereading it they committed it to memory and so carried the book around with them in their bosoms. Because of this, in a few months they attributed so much learning to themselves that they did not blush to dispute about the faith and the Gospel, not only with laypeople of the Catholic party, but with priests and monks, and furthermore, even with Masters and Doctors of Sacred Theology. Nay, more—even mere women were found who of their own accord dared to challenge the proposed themes and published books of the Germans—and that indeed they did by most boldly insulting men, reproaching them with ignorance, and holding them in contempt. And not only laymen and private citizens; but even certain Doctors, and licensed members of the faculty of Theology, and even whole universities.[34]

Versions from Luther's German

Before tracing the Luther Bible into other languages we must mention their co-dependence on Latin. However, this was not the Vulgate but rather the Latin text of Erasmus; in his first published New Testament were the Vulgate Latin, the Greek, and his Greek-supported Latin text. With Luther's German alongside Erasmus's three-column New Testament, urgent and excited translators into their own tongues would not stray far from the truth.

Dutch

There was, almost inevitably, a Dutch-language Luther Bible,[35] printed by Nicolaes Biestkens van Diest in Emden in 1558 and again in 1560. This Dutch Luther Bible was the first Dutch Bible with verse numbers. The Biestkens Bible continued in print into the eighteenth century, much used in Europe and North America by Baptists and Mennonites as well as Lutherans.

Danish

The most prolific use of the Luther Bible in translation was in the Scandinavian lands. Denmark and Sweden were united from 1380 to 1814 (although not always on friendly terms). They

Hans Tausen

shared the Danish language as the common tongue; there was clear likeness also to Norwegian. A Danish New Testament by Hans Mikkelsen had appeared at Leipzig in 1524. German mingled with Danish made this text uncouth, and a better translation by Christen Pedersen was printed at Antwerp in 1529 and 1531. The Danish Reformer Hans Tausen translated the Pentateuch from Luther's version, published in Magdeburg in 1535. The first complete Bible in Danish was published in 1550 at Copenhagen, very closely following Luther's version; a new edition came in 1589 and was reprinted in 1633. Finally there came a translation from the original languages by Hans Paulsen Resen in 1607. It was revised in 1647, and even after the separation of Sweden and Denmark it continued in use for another thirty or forty years.

Sheer delight moves me to extend the story of the Luther-based Danish Bibles to include Greenland and the Egedes. Hans (1686–1758) and Paul (1708–1789) Egede were father and son missionaries from Denmark. Paul was born in Greenland, where his father worked amongst the Eskimo people despite the general perception in Denmark that Eskimos were barbarous, near savage illiterates. Hans mastered the spoken Eskimo tongue, and Paul became fluent. While studying in Copenhagen Paul learned of a smallpox outbreak in

The Scriptures in Swedish being presented to Gustav Vasa

Greenland, and hearing that his mother had died there resolved to return to help his father. Hans never recovered his strength and returned to Denmark. Paul travelled laboriously, preaching as he went and gathering all available help to translate the Scriptures. He compiled an Eskimo dictionary and wrote a grammar, then translated the whole New Testament. This story was much repeated as the Reformation and Bible work rippled out across the world.

Swedish

Gustav Vasa became king of Sweden in 1523 and in due course rejected Romanism for Protestantism. He desired a Swedish edition of the Scriptures and asked Archbishop Johannes Magni of Uppsala for help with a translation of the New Testament. One of his bishops, Hans Brask of Linköping, a strict Romanist, declared that it would be better for the Apostle Paul to have been burned, than to be known by everyone. So much for *Sola Scriptura*!

But the Lord had His servants prepared: the New Testament was translated into Swedish from Luther's German by Laurentius Andreae and Olaus Petri and published at Stockholm in 1526. The whole Bible, similarly translated following Luther by Lars Petri, brother of Olaus, appeared in 1540–1541. The Petri brothers had met Luther and Melanchthon whilst studying in Wittenberg; Olaus was later instrumental in Laurentius Andreae's conversion from Catholicism. Olaus and Laurentius were together sentenced to death in 1540, reasons unknown, but after much popular pleading and the payment of heavy fines they were released. The Gustav Vasa Bible was for a very long time the church Bible of Sweden.

Finnish

Now back to the Baltic, where the Luther Bible travelled to the northernmost shore: Finland. Mikael Agricola's translation of the New Testament was the first part of the Bible translated into Finnish (*Se Wsi Testamenti Somexi:* 'The New Testament in Finnish'). Agricola, now regarded as the father of literary Finnish, had started work on the translation while he was studying in Germany between 1536 and 1539; it was

Mikael Agricola translating the Scriptures

published in 1548. He also translated parts of the Old Testament. These translations were based on a now familiar ground: the Luther Bible, the Vulgate, Erasmus's Greek and Latin New Testament, and the extra help of the 1541 Gustav Vasa Bible. A whole Bible in Finnish was published in 1642, the work of a bishop-led Evangelical Lutheran committee, and revised between 1683 and 1685. Bearing the simple title Biblia, it is generally referred to as the Old Church Bible, and is still in use by some. Don't these patterns keep appearing?

Agricola's 1548 Finnish New Testament

---

33. See *Quarterly Record* no. 579, April to June 2007, pp. 8–15.

34. *Lives: Two contemporary accounts of Martin Luther,* trans. by Elizabeth Vandiver, Ralph Keen and Thomas D. Frazel (Manchester, England: Manchester University Press, 2002), p. 106. Johann Cochlaeus was a German humanist and controversialist (1479–1552).

35. Ask a Dutch linguist just when Low German became High Dutch.

7: Geneva: John Calvin 1509–1564

John Calvin, born Jean Cauvin at Noyon in northern France, clearly belongs to the second generation of the Reformers: at the time of his birth in 1509 Erasmus was fifty-three, Luther was twenty-three and Farrell was twenty. Because of family connections, and destined for the ecclesiastical life, young Calvin received financial help from the Roman Catholic Church from the age of twelve. Technically he was an absentee holder of various church posts and offices, keeping them until 1534 when he disconnected from all such things. At fourteen he was sent to the University of Paris and enrolled in the extremely traditional Collège Montaigu[36]—resolutely hostile first to humanism and now to Luther. (Perhaps this was why Ignatius of Loyola went there in 1534. What a trio over forty years at the same college—Erasmus, Calvin and Loyola:[37] humanist, Reformer and counter-Reformer, and yet all scholars, and thorough, joyous Latinists!)

Collège Montaigu, Paris

In 1527 parental directives moved Calvin to study civil law instead of theology. Whatever agenda his father had in this, it shaped John Calvin's whole approach to the texts and methods of study. He learned the careful assessment of vocabulary, syntax, sentence structure and chain of reasoning in the written document—some not always designed to be clear. This was evident providential preparation for his life and work in Geneva with the text of Scripture, divinely intended to instruct and reveal.

Holbein's painting of a younger John Calvin

Calvin's change of course took him from Paris to Orléans and Bourges, where his enthusiasm for his legal studies led to long, health-sapping hours of study. He became a brilliant student and acknowledged humanist. He found time to acquire Greek there from the German Melchior Volmar, who had studied Greek in Paris around 1521 and edited several Greek grammars.

Calvin was still a Romanist, but began to associate with humanist friends before returning to Paris in 1531–1532, and found that the pressure of the Roman church on humanists and evangelical reformers was becoming intense. There, as he tells us in the introduction to his *Commentary on Psalms*,

> ...since I was too obstinately devoted to the superstitions of Popery to be easily extricated from so profound an abyss of mire, God by a sudden conversion subdued and brought my mind to a teachable frame, which was more hardened in such matters than might have been expected from one at my early period of life. Having thus received some taste and knowledge of true godliness I was immediately inflamed with so intense a desire to make progress therein, that although I did not altogether leave off other studies, I yet pursued them with less ardour. I was quite surprised to find that before a year had elapsed, all who had any desire after purer doctrine were continually coming to me to learn, although I myself was as yet but a mere novice and tyro.[38]

This unexpected role of teacher and counsellor brought trouble. Nicolas Cop, new rector of the University of Paris, took the Beatitudes (Matthew 5.3–11) as the text for his inaugural sermon on 1 November 1533 (All Saints' Day), declaring:

> The Law mentions the mercy of God, but only on a condition: provided the Law be fulfilled. The Gospel freely offers forgiveness of sins and justification. We have in fact not been accepted by God because of the Law's demands, but only because of the promise of Christ; if a man doubt this promise, he cannot live a godly life and is preparing himself for the fires of hell.[39]

Calvin was the obvious source of such doctrine and was certainly thought by many to have written it himself. Cop fled to Basel. Calvin remained in Paris under an assumed name—Charles d'Espeville.

In the spring of 1534 he travelled through France, now under his own name again. There came more trouble in Paris with the *affair des placards* on 17 October. During this Affair of the Placards,[40] anti-Catholic posters attacking the Roman mass appeared overnight in public places in Paris and other towns. One such placard was actually placed on the bedchamber door of King Francis I, putting an end to his conciliatory policies towards not only the Protestant reformers but all protesters. It also meant a quick departure to Strasbourg for Calvin, where he paused briefly, then on to Basel.

Basel, in north-west Switzerland on the River Rhine, close to the country's borders with France and Germany, had long been a centre of humanist printing. It was a crossroads and meeting place for many reformers, who were of firm but not always the same view of the issues that faced them. Erasmus had frequented the city since 1516, returning there in 1535 before Calvin came in January 1536; in July Erasmus died.

A 1532 first edition of Calvin's **Institutes of the Christian Religion**

The first edition of Calvin's *Institutes of Christian Religion* was printed in Basel that same year. In his 'Prefatory Address to King Francis I of France' Calvin assured the monarch that,

> When I first engaged in this work, nothing was farther from my thoughts than to write what should afterwards be presented to your Majesty. My intention was only to furnish a kind of rudiments, by which those who feel some interest in religion might be trained to true godliness. And I toiled at the task chiefly for the sake of my countrymen the French, multitudes of whom I perceived to be hungering and thirsting after Christ, while very few seemed to have been duly imbued with even a slender knowledge of him. That this was the object which I had in view is apparent from the work itself, which is written in a simple and elementary form adapted for instruction.[41]

Amongst other labours, Calvin studied Hebrew and produced prefaces to the French editions of the Bible produced by Pierre Robert Olivétan, his cousin. This was, however, not the first edition of the French Bible. That distinction belonged to Jacques Lefèvre d'Étaples, who prepared the first French Bible translations, which were printed in Antwerp: the New Testament in 1523, the Old Testament in 1528 and the whole Bible in 1530. This work was done from the Latin Vulgate, but revised and improved in 1535 by Olivétan. Olivétan used the Greek and Hebrew received texts, and accompanied the work with many scholarly notes. Calvin wrote the Latin preface for Olivétan, and the Bible was published at Neuchatel in Switzerland. Calvin published his 1540 revision of the Bible in Geneva.

Calvin and Olivétan

There were many others involved in French Bible production, but the most significant in Bible history is that of 1553, printed by Robert Stephens (also known as Estienne or Stephanus), with the first appearance of the now familiar chapter and verse divisions. This in turn was revised and republished in 1558 by Calvin's

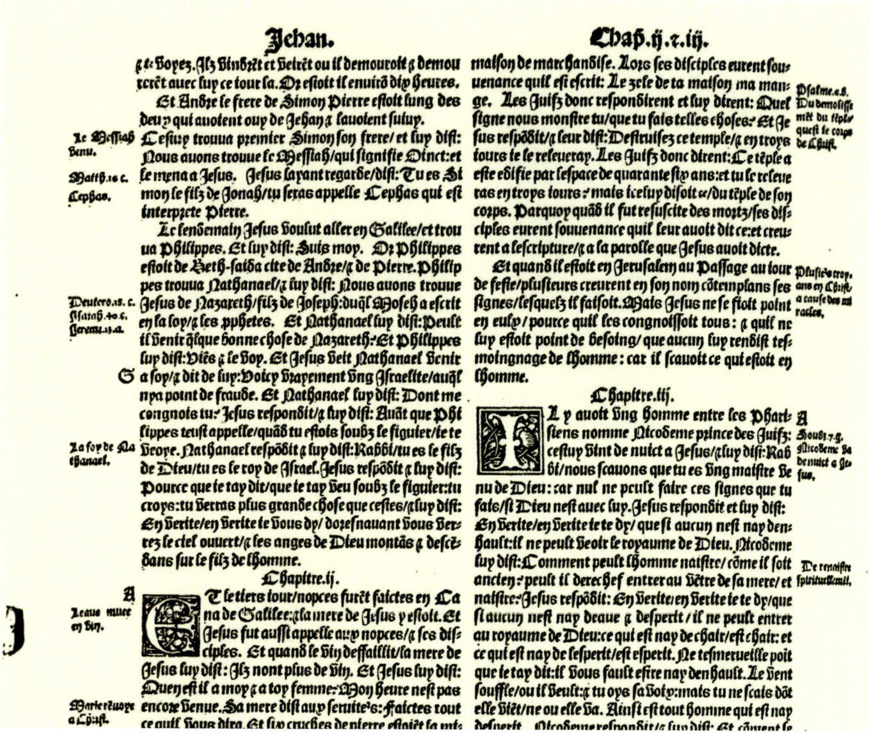

A sample from John's Gospel chapters 2 and 3 in Olivétan's 1535 French Bible

successor in Geneva, Theodore Beza, becoming the 'definitive' French Geneva Bible. This Olivétan-Calvin-Beza Bible was revised by David Martin, a native of Languedoc, around the beginning of the eighteenth century.

Once the *Institutes* were 'put to bed', as printers call it, Calvin journeyed into Lombardy, northern Italy, where Renée of France,[42] the younger surviving child of Louis XII of France, lived. She was Duchess of Ferrara by her marriage to Ercole II d'Este, a grandson of Pope Alexander VI. The Duchess had become an important supporter of the Protestant Reformation and invited Calvin to her court. She was in correspondence with large numbers of Protestants abroad.

In May 1536 Calvin returned to Basel and decided to go again into France where persecution seemed to be less. In his home country he could also attend to his affairs and visit his siblings, Antoine and Marie. With them he set out for Strasbourg where there was a thriving French community in exile.

Troop movements obliged them to change course. They decided to spend just one night in Geneva, on 8 August 1536, but William Farel, already resident in Geneva, thought otherwise. In the course of characteristically blunt and forceful urgings, which he foisted upon Calvin to assume ministry in Geneva, Farel laid upon him the stout imprecation, which Calvin ever remembered, that 'God would curse my retirement and the tranquillity of the studies which I sought if I would withdraw and refuse to give assistance when the necessity was so urgent'. Calvin was shamed, or terrified, into staying.

And so at the age of twenty-seven John Calvin came to Geneva. As well as the theological, confessional[43] and commentary tradition of that time and place, for Bible historians and students sixteenth-century Geneva became the foot of a rainbow for Bible versions which have given an enduring legacy.

Regarding the tradition of Bibles produced in Geneva it was stated in a preface to the English Geneva Bible of 1560:

> …the Word of God is an evident token of God's love and our assurance of his defence, wheresoever it is obediently received; it is the trial of the spirits; and as the prophet says, It is a fire and hammer to break the stony heart of them that resist God's mercies offered by the preaching of the same. Yea, it is sharper than any two-edged sword to examine the very thoughts and to judge the affections of the heart, and to discover whatsoever lies hid under hypocrisy and would be secret from the face of God and his church.[44]

The skyline of modern Geneva: still prominent is the Cathedral of St. Pierre, the setting for much of Calvin's ministry

The English Geneva Bible first published in 1560 was to be reprinted several times and continued in use among English-speaking peoples across the globe well into the seventeenth century. But more of this later!

---

36. Many sources say Montaigne, but that was not established until the nineteenth century.

37. Ignatius of Loyola (1491–1556) was a Spanish priest and theologian who in 1539 founded the Jesuit movement in Roman Catholicism.

38. John Calvin, Preface to *Commentary on Psalms*, Arthur Golding, trans., on *Christian Classics Ethereal Library*, www.ccel.org/ccel/calvin/calcom08.vi.html.

39. Methuen, Luther and Calvin, p. 119.

40. Subtitled 'Genuine articles on the horrific, great and unbearable abuses of the papal mass, invented directly contrary to the Holy Supper of our Lord, sole mediator and sole saviour Jesus Christ.' In response the king publicly declared himself a Roman Catholic.

41. John Calvin, ***Institutes of the Christian Religion,*** Henry Beveridge, trans. *Christian Classic Ethereal Library*, www.ccel.org/ccel/calvin/institutes.txt.

42. Her anguished story would be worth telling at large; brought to the local inquisition by her husband and tried for heresy, resisting all pressure until her two daughters were taken from her. Calvin's last letter was to Renée. Do seek more detail elsewhere.

43. Confessionalism: an agreed and defined system of beliefs, doctrines and practices at the same time distinguishing and yet dividing the evangelical groups. Luther had sorrowfully anticipated this.

44. Epistle Dedicatory 'to the most virtuous and noble Queen Elizabeth, Queen of England, France, and Ireland, &c.' *A Reformation Guide to Scripture: The Prologues from the Geneva Bible 1560* (Edinburgh, Scotland: Banner of Truth Trust, 2010).

8: Europe: Other Reformation-era Bibles

Italian

Giovanni Diodati (1576–1649) was the first translator of the Bible into Italian from Hebrew and Greek sources, and renowned in his generation as an eloquent preacher. He considered himself an Italian *di nation lucchese* (of the Lucca nation in Tuscany) although born at Geneva, Switzerland, where his family took refuge as Protestant refugees. The Diodatis were part of the so-called 'Italian Cabal' group of families, emigrants in Geneva.

Giovanni matriculated at the Genevan Academy in 1596, and at age twenty-one was nominated professor of Hebrew there, recommended by Theodore Beza. In 1608 he was made a pastor, and the next year succeeded Beza as professor of theology. In 1618–1619 he attended the Synod of Dort, being one of the six appointed to draw up the Canons of Dort. In 1645 Diodati resigned his professorship; he died at Geneva on 3 October 1649. Diodati's chief fame is as translator of the Bible into Italian (1603, edited with notes 1607). He also undertook a French translation of the Bible in 1644, and among his other works are his *Annotationes in Biblia* (1607) with an English translation (*Pious and Learned Annotations upon the Holy Bible*) published in London in 1648.

Giovanni Diodati depicted in a 1647 engraving by Wenceslas Hollar; taken from an English translation of Diodati's* Pious and Learned Annotations upon the Holy Bible. *The inscription reads:

Reader look well on Diodati, more
Upon the Golden work he stands before
Lest in Scriptures Labyrinth thy mind
Should snare and lose itself, here thou mayest find
A Clue that will through each mysterious story
Lead thee from earth up to the throne of Glory,
Where thy well-guided soul shall once meet his
Who here directs thee to eternal bliss.

Dutch Versions

Dutch Protestantism encompassed Lutherans, Mennonites, and Reformed, leading to the production of various versions. The Lutherans had Biestkens's version, the first Dutch edition with verse divisions, as mentioned above; the

Mennonites and Baptists used this version also. Reformed congregations had a Bible based on Zwingli's Zurich Bible of 1548–1549: an edition which was not without plain dependence on Luther and others.

By 1594 the States General was determined to provide a thorough revision. This was to give us the Staatenbibel or Staatenvertaaling. Associated with this is the name of Philips van Marnix, a Flemish and Dutch statesman, writer, and probably author of the 'Het Wilhelmus', the Dutch National anthem. In Dutch he was Filips van Marnix, heer van Sint-Aldegonde, heer van West-Souburg; in French, Philippe de Marnix, seigneur de Sainte-Aldegonde; and in English, Philips of Marnix, Lord of Saint-Aldegonde, Lord of West-Souburg. He was born in Brussels in 1540 and died in Leiden in December 1598.

Marnix studied theology with Calvin and Beza in Geneva, returning to the Netherlands in 1560, and was at the first meeting of the States-General Assembly at Dordrecht in 1572, representing his master, William, Prince of Orange. He, with an assistant, was entrusted in 1596 (just two years before Marnix died) with the task of a new translation. The Synod of Dort deliberated over the translation, and the translation itself was finally completed in 1632, with revisions continuing until 1635. The first edition was printed, with and without notes, in 1636, but not published until July 1637. Only the English Authorised Version can compare with the Staatenvertaaling for weight of distribution and impact around the world through trade and settlement.[45]

Spanish Versions

Early fifteenth-century Castilian manuscript versions of the Old Testament were made by Sephardic Jews[46] from the Hebrew text and in the order of the Hebrew canon.[47] The first printed Bible text in Spanish was the New Testament translated by Francis of Enzinas in Antwerp in 1543. Francisco de Enzinas[48] (1518–1552) was a classical scholar, translator, author and Protestant. Family connections in the Low Countries, a familiar pattern at that time, took him there in 1536 to master commercial matters. By 1539 he had instead enrolled in the trilingual College of Louvain, part of Erasmus's heritage. His brother Diego joined him there, and they collaborated in a Spanish edition of Calvin's 1538 Catechism and Luther's *Freedom*

Title page of the 1553 Spanish Ferrara Bible

of the Christian Man. In October 1541 Enzinas went to Wittenberg to study with Melanchthon, and there he completed the New Testament in Spanish. This had a marked influence on all following translations, including the Reina-Valera version—the standard Bible of the Protestant Spanish-speaking world.

In 1553 the Ferrara Bible appeared: a Ladino (Hebrew-Spanish) version of the Hebrew Bible (our Old Testament). This translation closely followed Hebrew syntax rather than that of the everyday Ladino, and is written entirely in the Latin alphabet (with necessary diacritical marks for Ladino pronunciation). We mention this because Casiodoro de Reina plainly acknowledges use of it in his Bible translation.

Casiodoro de Reina was born about 1520 in the Province of Badajoz, and studied the Bible from his youth. By 1557 he was a monk in the Monastery of St. Isidore, Seville, but at that time he encountered Lutheranism and became a Protestant. Reina fled, along with other monks suspected by the Office of the Inquisition of holding Protestant tendencies, to John Calvin's Geneva.

The Ladino (Judaeo-Spanish) Ferrara translation of the Old Testament was a basis for the 1569 Spanish Casiodoro de Reina translation. As de Reina said,

> Of the old Spanish translation of the Old Testament, published in Ferrara, we have availed ourselves hereof more than any other that we have seen thus far, not simply due to it always being accurate in such things, but rather because **it gives us the natural and first meaning of Hebrew terms, and the differences between the tenses of the verbs as found in the same text;** it is a work that is worthy of greater esteem (in the judgement of all those that understand it) than the many others found to this day: and by this exceptional aid, of which the other translations have not taken advantage, we hope that ours will not be considered inferior to any of them.

'Ferrara Bible', *Wikipedia*, en.wikipedia.org/wiki/Ferrara_Bible [emphasis added]

In 1558, however, Reina declared that Geneva had become a new Rome and left for London, where he served as pastor to Spanish Protestant refugees. King Philip II of Spain was outraged, and in April 1562 the Inquisition in Seville burned an image of Casiodoro de Reina. His works were placed in the Index of prohibited books and he was declared a 'heresiarch' (leader of heretics).

While in exile in London, Antwerp, Frankfurt, Orléans and Bergerac, Reina began translating the Bible into Spanish. He used a number of works as source texts: the Ferrara Bible with comparisons to the Masoretic Text and the Old Latin, the Textus Receptus of Erasmus, and the translation of Francisco de Enzinas. Reina's Spanish translation was published in Geneva in 1569. Still more Lutheran than Genevan, Reina published a catechism in the style of Luther's, in Latin, French and Dutch. He died in 1594 in Frankfurt am Main.

Cipriano de Valera (c. 1532–c. 1600) was born at Fregenal de la Sierra near Seville but was in exile in England during most of the long reign of Queen Elizabeth I. He

Cipriano de Valera

edited the first major revision of Reina's Spanish Bible. Published in 1602 this Bible continues to this day, even after revisions, as the Reina-Valera version. Valera also edited a Spanish edition of Calvin's *Institutes*. From 1559 he was a professor at the University of Cambridge, and in 1560 was made a fellow of Magdalene College, Cambridge.

The chain connecting Bible and Reformation has many unexpected and surprising links. John Thomson, an Englishman trading in Spain in the seventeenth century, was denounced there as possessing a Spanish Bible, and his house was searched by the Inquisition. The Bible was there, in full view, in a room which the Inquisition 'chose' not to enter. John left Spain and settled near Barnstaple in the west of England, where his son George was born in 1698. George became vicar of a church in a small village, but served the world as a forerunner of the Evangelical Awakening in Cornwall before Whitefield was converted and ten years before the Wesleys arrived.

Hungarian Versions

János Erdosi 's 1541 New Testament

Manuscript portions exist which were made by Franciscan friars suspected of having Hussite sympathies. The first printed book in Hungarian (Magyar) was the epistles of Paul, made from the Vulgate and printed in Poland in 1533. This was followed in 1541 by a New Testament translated from Greek by János Erdosi, a pupil of Melanchthon. The printing press used had to be under the protection of a Hungarian nobleman.

Gáspár Károli

The outstanding name in Hungarian Bible scholarship is Gáspár Károli (1529–1591), born in Hungary[49] to a Serbian family who were refugees from the Ottoman incursion into Europe. His birth name, Gáspár Radicsics, reflects the Serbian connection, although the family became Hungarian Protestants. Károli went to the Halle and Wittenberg Academy in 1556, became a pastor in Hungary, and is still the most widely known and famous Hungarian Calvinist. By 1586 he had translated the Bible into Hungarian, the first complete Hungarian translation of the Bible. When printing began, the final text was not complete so Károli's manuscript was taken page by page to the printer

Bálint Mantskovit by students at Gönc. It was finally published in Vizsoly in 1590. A copy of the Károli Bible is on display in the Reformed church of Vizsoly village.

The Reformed Church in the village of Vizsoly, north-east Hungary

The 1566 Synod of Gönc (Göncz) had directed 'Let every minister have, if it is possible, his own Bible', and also that 'the reading of the Bible be the most frequent work every day for the minister'. Friend and fellow-labourer to Károli in all this work was Albert Szenczi Molnár, a Calvinist pastor, linguist, philosopher, poet, religious writer and translator. Molnár had an enduring impact on Hungarian literature, both prose and verse; his works include Psalm translations, revised editions of the Vizsoly/Károli Bible, Calvin's *Institutes* and the Heidelberg Catechism.

45. Although the Geneva Bible was the Puritan favourite, and flourished in North America especially.

46. The Hebrew word *sepharad* relates to Spain, where many Jews were settled. Moors were more accommodating than Christians.

47. The Hebrew Old Testament divides and orders the books into three groups: *Torah* (Genesis to Deuteronomy), *Nevi'im* (Joshua, Judges, Samuel, Kings, Isaiah, Jeremiah, Ezekiel, Hosea to Malachi), and *Ketuvim* (Psalms, Proverbs, Job, Song of Songs, Ruth, Lamentations, Ecclesiastes, Esther, Daniel, Ezra, Nehemiah, Chronicles).

48. Enzinas played games with his name, calling himself Francis Dryander, from the Greek *drus*, an oak, which can then be *encina* in Spanish.

49. Some sources say Romania.

9: London-Oxford-Cambridge: the English Reformation

This cumbersome heading gives a clue to the complicated nature of the Reformation in England. I reduce it to an alarming simplicity.

In London Henry VIII blundered into a political rearrangement of the nation's relationship with the papacy to protect his purpose of securing a male heir, however many marriages and divorces that took. He never ceased to think of himself as a good Catholic, indeed as Defender of the Faith. This title was granted to Henry VIII by the pope in 1521, when the king criticised Martin Luther in print.[50] It led to the FD, *Fid. Def.*, on English coinage.

'I felt a marvellous comfort and quietness, insomuch that my bruised bones lept for joy, Psal. 51:8. After this, the Scripture began to be more pleasant unto me than the honey or the honeycomb; wherein I learned that all my labours, my fasting and watching, all the redemption of masses and pardons, being done without truth in Christ, who alone saveth his people from their sins; these I say, I learned to be nothing else but even, as St. Augustine saith, a hasty and swift running out of the right way'.

Thomas Bilney
after reading 1 Timothy 1.15

In the universities, what we might call a real reformation had been fermenting for some time, and familiar names begin to appear. Erasmus had visited Cambridge and Thomas Bilney was captivated by his Greek New Testament. Bilney was awakened and converted in reading 1 Timothy 1.15, and became part of a joyful group meeting behind locked doors at the White Horse Inn. Perhaps it stirred some connection with the fourteenth-century Lollards or the later Hussites, with true Christian congregations meeting only in Christ's name. The White Horse Inn group included Thomas Cranmer, Hugh Latimer, Robert Barnes, Miles Coverdale, Matthew Parker, William Tyndale and John Rogers, as well as others whose names are less familiar to us. What a truly potent gathering.

William Tyndale

William Tyndale (1494–1536)[51] is well known amongst the Reformers particularly for producing the first New Testament in English

Tyndale's New Testament

translated directly from the Greek. It proved to be a translation which would influence English Scriptures for centuries to come; indeed, it is estimated that nearly ninety per cent of the Authorised Version's New Testament is from Tyndale.

Tyndale obtained a copy of Luther's German New Testament and was moved to abandon the Latin and produce English Scriptures from the Biblical language texts as Luther had done. Tyndale sought permission to do his work in England, but persecution sent him to the Continent. His New Testament was completed and published in Worms in 1526; copies soon found their way to England where it received official, but not popular, condemnation. Tyndale managed to produce two revisions of his New Testament and translate parts of the Old Testament. But the long arm of Romanism and the English crown found him, and in 1536 he was betrayed and martyred. Tyndale's dying words are reported to have been 'Lord! Open the king of England's eyes', a prayer answered just a few years later with Henry VIII's proclamation that an English Bible be prepared and copies placed in each church throughout the realm.

Erasmus had also visited Oxford, making great friends of John Colet and Thomas More. Tyndale had done a first degree at Oxford, as did John Foxe (who was later to write *Actes and Monuments*…—popularly known as *Foxe's Book of Martyrs*). In 1527 Archbishop Warham, as chancellor of the university, wrote to Cardinal Wolsey complaining that Oxford had 'no small number of young and incircumspect fools'[52] tainted with Reformation principles.

Edward VI

'O Gracious God and most Merciful Father,
Who hast given us the rich and precious jewel of thy holy word:
Assist us with thy Spirit,
That it may be written in our hearts to our everlasting comfort,
To re-form us according to thine own image,
And increase in us all heavenly virtues:
For Jesus Christ's sake.'

Edward VI (1537–1553)

Peter Martyr Vermigli was an Italian Reformed theologian who fled from Italy and at Cranmer's request came to Oxford to be Regius Professor of Divinity. He became much involved with the Book of Common Prayer in the hopeful but short reign of Edward VI.

Edward, born in 1537 the long-hoped-for son of Henry VIII, was raised under Protestant guidance.

He came to the throne in 1547, aged nine. In his short reign Protestantism was established in England. Before he died in 1553 he appointed a cousin, Lady Jane Grey, to be his successor. Cranmer buried King Edward in accord with the Book of Common Prayer and Lady Jane became queen for nine days, but it proved to be an unsuccessful attempt to exclude the aggressively Roman Catholic princess Mary from the throne. Mary was proclaimed queen in July 1553 and Lady Jane went to the scaffold on 12 February 1554.

Mary was the daughter of Catherine of Aragon and Henry VIII. Mary's husband was Philip II of Roman Catholic Spain, and her adherence to the faith brought her the sobriquet 'Catholic Mary'. The queen's toll of Protestants executed under her reign led to 'Bloody Mary' as her defining nickname. It was a woeful time for reform in England. Many hundreds of English Protestants fled to the continent during Mary's reign. They settled in Protestant countries: the Netherlands,[53] Switzerland and Germany, but also in France, Italy and Poland. A few went to Scotland and the Scandinavian countries—Denmark particularly. Where it was possible they joined with reformed churches, and often formed their own congregations.

Mary I

These exiles did not plan to remain on the Continent for long, being troubled as to the legitimacy of their flight. Should they have stayed to face persecution? During their Continental stay few of the exiles integrated well with their new communities. They did have some financial support from London merchants, as well from the King of Denmark, the Prince Palatine of the Rhine and others. Heinrich Bullinger, Konrad Pellikan and other leaders of the Continental reform movement helped in practical ways too.

Differences broke out between the exiles about church order, government, discipline and forms of worship—they plainly presaged Queen Elizabeth's later struggle to maintain a grip on 'her' English church. The English congregation in Strasbourg, whose leaders and membership included names to become prominent later in the English church (Myles Coverdale—England to Geneva via Denmark—made several visits), ordered its affairs in accord with the 1552 Book of Common Prayer. John Knox stepped in to provide a compromise. His forms and standards were printed in 1556 as

John Knox

the Book of Geneva. From 1564 to 1645 this was in official use in the Church of Scotland, and became the basis for the modern Book of Common Order used by Presbyterian churches.

In Frankfurt, with the help of a local magistrate and the use of a vacant church building, another group of English exiles met, who preferred a reformed liturgy drawn up by William Whittingham, which was based on the models of Zwingli and Calvin. A dedicated in-house college or Bible school was established by the congregation, teaching Hebrew, Greek and theology. This Frankfurt congregation saw itself as the proper pattern of Protestantism abroad and soon, surely, back home.

However, the root problem—the struggle between the Anglican and Presbyterian views—lasted for the next one hundred years.

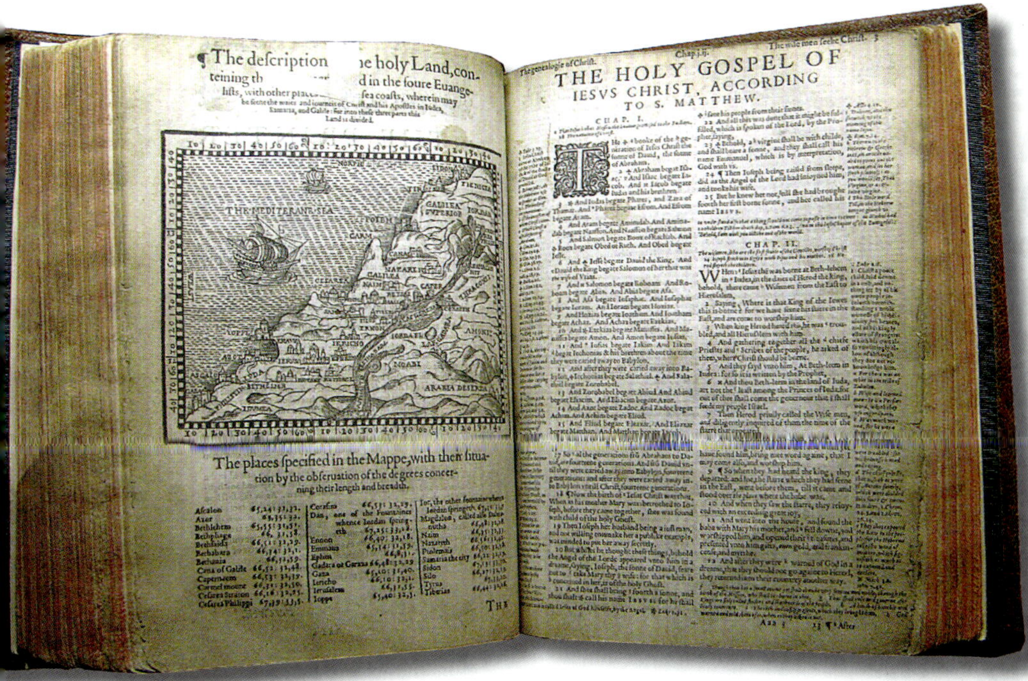

A 1560 edition of the Geneva Bible

English Geneva Bible

The English-language Geneva Bible[54] was perhaps the most powerful instrument of reform to appear in the sixteenth century, but was not the first English Bible from the Biblical languages. William Tyndale's delightfully enthusiastic and groundbreaking New Testament had appeared in print in 1526.[55] It was a product of his conversion to Christ by the spiritual impact of the 1516 Erasmus Greek New Testament. Tyndale also translated the Old Testament from Hebrew into English; the Pentateuch was published 1530, Joshua to Chronicles plus Jonah in 1537.[56] Coverdale completed and published a whole Bible in English in 1535, resurfacing as Matthew's Bible in 1537; then the Great Bible in 1539 (Cromwell's) and 1540 (Cranmer's). The Geneva exiles were aware of these, and of opposition to them from church and crown.

An English New Testament appeared in Geneva in June 1557. This was quite different from all that had gone before in English, and especially from the Great Bibles of 1539 and 1540. It was small, printed in a fine Roman typeface on carefully selected paper, and well laid out. Verses were numbered in the pattern of Stephens's 1551 Greek New Testament. Words not in the Greek Testament but thought necessary for the clear understanding of the text were included in italic type. Sounds familiar, doesn't it? This appeared without a name but is now known to be William Whittingham's work.

The English Geneva Bible appeared in 1560: compact, with numbered verses set out in two columns, and notes that amounted to a Biblical encyclopaedia. This product of learning, printing mastery and thoroughgoing commitment to Biblical scholarship became the people's Bible throughout that century and well into the next. It was, and still is, maligned, even by those who should know better, but sought out still by those who do know better. This Bible finished the task of completing the translation of the Old Testament from Hebrew to English; Tyndale's work had only taken such work to the end of Chronicles.

The next English Bible chronologically was the Bishops' in 1568. As a response to the Geneva it scarcely registered at all, and as furthering the work of reform it was a failure.

Let the Geneva have the last word here:

> ...considering how hard a thing it is to vnderstand the holy Scripture, and what errors, sects and heresies growe dailie for lacke of the true knollage thereof, and how many are discouraged (as thei pretend) because thei cannot atteine to the true and simple meaning of the same, we haue also endeuored bothe by the diligent reading of the best commentaries, and also by the conference with the godly and learned brethren, to gather brief annotations vpon all the hard places, aswel for the vnderstanding of suche wordes as are obscure, and for the declaration of the text, as for the application of the same as may most apperteine to Gods glorie and the edification of his Churche.[57]

The English church in Geneva was, of course, where the Geneva Bible was produced—the most popular English version of the era and notorious for its annotations supporting Reformed theology and active resistance.

In the building in Geneva where Calvin delivered lectures—later styled the Calvin Auditory—Calvin proposed that English services should be held. This practice continues in the building still, now under the Church of Scotland.

zabeth I in her coronation robes

Meanwhile, turning our attention back to England, it is tempting to see the royal, top-down, political reform and the university 'incircumspect fools' as clearly distinguishable. They were not. They were intertwined like lichens and vines. The university men returning from the Continent soon held office in what was really Henry's 'independent catholic church', and the Calvinist-Arminian, Lutheran-Catholic, Episcopalian Anglican Church happened. Elizabeth I found the all-inclusive church ideally suited to her view of Protestant Britain and the Middle Way between the Protestants and Roman Catholics. Not all of her subjects did. Only the Protestants wanted her to be queen, but even for many of them this was reform not carried through: cut off, inadequately formed, still without form and void. They wanted the English church to be purified of all vestiges of Romanism. Among them were the Puritans, at first within the church, but soon seceding and dividing among themselves.

50. The title was revoked when Henry broke with Rome in 1530, but not until 1544 by the English Parliament.

51. For more information on Tyndale see David Allen, '*William Tyndale: The Apostle of England*', *Quarterly Record* no. 614, January to March 2016, pp. 26–32.

52. Warham wrote to Wolsey, 'Thinks it a pity that a small number of "incircumspect fools" should endanger the whole university with the charge of Lutheranism' (Calig. B. VI. 171*. B. M. Ellis, 3 Ser. I.239. 8 March 1521).

53. There was an English Reformed Church in Amsterdam.

54. I have lightly depended on a download of Professor Daniell's lecture given at the Geneva Tyndale Conference in October 2001. Also my copies of Lewis Lupton's early (1962) articles on the Geneva in the *Free Grace Record* magazine

55. The 1525 exists only as a lonely fragment, survivor of the vicious destruction of the printed sheets.

56. Now accessible as *Tyndale's Old Testament*, a modern spelling edition edited by David Daniell (New Haven, CT, USA: Yale University Press, 1992).

57. 'Preface to the Geneva Bible', in Gerald Hammond, *The Making of the English Bible* (Manchester, England: Carcanet, 1988), p. 89.

10: Bibles and Reformation in the British Isles

Before pursuing that thread we must look around other centres, with other languages, their own martyrs, their own Bibles, within the British Isles.

Wales

Welsh is a Celtic language used today by about three-quarters of a million people in Wales (Cymru) and in the Welsh colony (yr Wladfa) in Patagonia. There are also Welsh speakers in England (Lloegr), Scotland (yr Alban), Canada, the USA (yr Unol Daleithiau), Australia (Awstralia) and New Zealand (Seland Newydd). At the beginning of the twentieth century about half of the population of Wales spoke Welsh as an everyday language; by 2011 the census showed only twenty-seven per cent saying that they spoke Welsh. Even in the later twentieth century the Welsh language had no legal status in Welsh affairs.

Two names stand out in connection with the Welsh Scriptures: Bishop William Morgan, Bible translator; and John Penry, Wales's most memorable martyr. The Reformation had no immediate impact in Wales, for Roman masses in Latin and Protestant sermons in English were equally meaningless to multitudes of natural Welsh speakers, not many of whom had reading skills even in their own tongue. Coverdale's Great Bible of 1539, chained for use in parish churches, met only apathy in Wales; it was in English. Queen Mary's incomprehensible mass-books generated the same general apathy amongst Welsh speakers as had Edward's equally non-Welsh prayer books.

What was to be done? Morgan and Penry were both Cambridge men, both contemporaries there of future Archbishop John Whitgift. Whitgift displayed a lifelong kindness to Morgan, but hounded Penry to execution.

John Penry was born in 1559 at Cefn Brith farm near Llangammarch, Brecknockshire. Matriculated at Peterhouse, Cambridge, in December 1580 he quickly became a convinced Protestant with strong Puritan leanings. Graduated B.A., he moved to St Alban's Hall, Oxford, becoming M.A. in July 1586, after which he was licensed as a university preacher.

Parliament made provision for translating the Bible into Welsh; the New Testament was issued in 1567. The print run was not sufficient to supply a copy for each parish church. Indignant of such negligence, Penry published in 1587 *The Equity of an Humble Supplication* in the behalf of the country of Wales, that some order may be taken for the preaching of the Gospel among those people. He poured out his grief: 'O destitute and forlorn condition! Preaching itself in many parts is unknown. In some places a sermon is read once in three months'. The 'idolatry and superstition' in Wales he blamed on the absence of learned ministers. 'Dumb ministers' they were called, restricted to reading approved prayers and homilies from the Book of Common Prayer. To address this problem he proposed a system of lay pastors supported in part with voluntary gifts from the people.

This rebuke of the practices of the Church of England won the undying enmity of Whitgift, who caused him to be brought instantly before the high commission and imprisoned for about a month for the 'heresy' of calling non-preaching ministers no true ministers. Eventually, on 21 May 1593 Penry was found guilty of treason and sentenced to death. His old Cambridge companion, Archbishop Whitgift, was first to sign his death warrant. He was hanged on the 29 May at the unusual hour of 4.00 p.m. Although described later as 'the morning star of Protestant nonconformity in Wales', his influence at the time was limited. He was probably, however, the first independent Puritan preacher in Wales.

William Morgan, unusually, studied Hebrew. His tutor was Antoine Rodolphe Chevallier (1523–1572), a French Protestant Hebraist who came to England in Edward VI's time. Chevallier was French tutor to the future Queen Elizabeth. During the reign of bloody Queen Mary he fled to Strasbourg, then travelled to Geneva as a friend of John Calvin. Chevallier returned to England in 1568 to plead Elizabeth's help for the Huguenots, eventually settling there and becoming Regius Professor of Hebrew at Cambridge.

Morgan met Chevallier in Cambridge. Hebrew study, with a little French, was immensely valuable to Morgan for his Welsh translation work. Returning to Wales, Morgan's abilities as a scholar attracted Richard Davies, who felt that Morgan should take up the task of translating the Old Testament, abandoned by himself and William Salesbury. In 1578 William Morgan was appointed

Bishop William Morgan

The title page of the 1588 Morgan Bible

vicar of Llanrhaeadr-ym-Mochnant in Denbighshire. He lived there until 1595, where he undertook the translation of the whole Bible. Whitgift appointed him Bishop of Llandaff (Cardiff), then in 1601 Bishop of St. Asaph. He died on 10 September 1604 and was buried inside the cathedral.

In his preface to Morgan's Welsh Bible of 1588, William Salesbury wrote

> Although it is much to be desired that the inhabitants of the same Island should be of the same speech and language, it must be equally borne in mind, that to effect this end so much time and trouble is required, that to be willing to suffer God's people **to perish in the meantime from hunger of His Word**, were both barbarous and cruel.[58]

Bible society work, and TBS—also unwilling that God's people should suffer from hunger of His Word in their own tongue—are derived from the impact of the Morgan Bible. The story of Mary Jones and her Bible does not need to be retold here, but it was her hunger for the Word of God in her own tongue that drove her in 1800 to walk the twenty-six miles to Bala and Thomas Charles. Charles's distress at being unable to meet the need was shared with ministers in London, and the seed of the British and Foreign Bible Society of 1804 was firmly planted. In 1831 a difference of opinion on the doctrine of the Trinity (alongside other issues) led to the formation of the Trinitarian Bible Society. Another link in the chain Bible-reformation-Bible is complete.

Other Gaelic Bibles in the British Isles

First chronologically was Erse, the Gaelic of Ireland. In 1602 a New Testament was produced in Dublin, using type presented by Elizabeth I, and in 1685 the Old Testament in Erse using type presented by Robert Boyle. Editions were printed in an Erse typeface and also in a Roman typeface, these being used also in Scotland until the Society in Scotland for Promoting Christian Knowledge (SSPCK) issued their own Gaelic New Testament in Edinburgh in 1767, Old Testament in 1801. The SSPCK had avoided use of the Gaelic language but soon saw that teaching pupils to read English only by rote, without understanding, did not further Christian knowledge. A Gaelic-English vocabulary book was produced in 1741, preparing the way for the 1767 New Testament.

Manx is the Gaelic tongue of the Isle of Man; Gospels and Acts appeared in Manx in 1763, with Romans to Revelation in 1767, all undertaken by the Society for Promoting Christian Knowledge (SPCK). The Manx Old Testament was produced by SPCK in 1771–1773 at Whitehaven, a convenient port for the Isle of Man. One of the translators, John Kelly, suffered shipwreck while carrying some manuscript pages to the Isle; he clambered onto the rock which had caused the wreck and held the papers above water level for five hours until rescued.

These Gaelic tongues were mutually intelligible, but not with Welsh nor with Breton—the language of Brittany in north-west France, which historically first seeded these languages either side of the Irish Sea. The TBS produced a New Testament in the Tréguier Breton dialect in 1883. The spiritual impact of these Scriptures in each Gaelic tongue is most evident in Wales and the Scottish Highlands.

Thinking of Scotland, it would be remiss to ignore the Haldane brothers in the context of this current study. Robert Haldane was born in 1764, James in 1768 in Perthshire; both were converted to Christ in the 1790s. Their evangelistic trips through the Highlands Islands and Borders of Scotland, accompanied at times by such notable men as Charles Simeon and Rowland Hill, were fruitful but antagonised the Church of Scotland.

Robert Haldane's visit to Geneva in 1816–1817 was highly significant. His private lectures to students on the book of Romans led to a number of conversions—much to the annoyed distress of their rationalistic professors. Those converted students included Merle D'Aubigné, Frederic Monod (brother of Adolphe, William and Horace, all pastors of *Le Réveil*—revival—in France), Cesar Malan and others.

Back home the Haldanes became involved in the 'apocrypha controversy', in which the British and Foreign Bible Society planned to produce and distribute Bibles with the Apocrypha. Robert was a vice-president of the Edinburgh arm of the BFBS, and took an anti-apocrypha stand. The end result was the withdrawal of all the Scottish societies, who later formed the National Bible Society of Scotland. Robert died in 1842, James in 1851, their lives and labours underlining that the link—Bible-Reformation-Bible—cannot become static.

58. Quoted in David Ross, *Wales: History of a Nation* (New Lanark, Scotland: Geddes and Grosset, 2008), p. 137 (emphasis mine).

11: Trento (Trent): the Counter Reformation

There had been scattered attempts throughout the sixteenth century to find a ground of positive discussion between Rome and the separating and splintering groups of reformers. In time the Roman Church rebounded. In response to the Reformation, the church called the Council of Trent, a series of meetings designed to address and counter the concerns brought by the Reformation. The meetings, in 1545–1547, 1551–1552 and 1562–1563, were held in Trento, capital town of Trentino: almost the most northerly region on the west side of the Italian peninsula, but just inside Austria and the Holy Roman Empire.[59] The Papal States, under the direct rule of the pope, provided a contiguous overland corridor, a long finger of territory from Rome to Trento: safe travelling then for the delegates, though Venice was not too far away for sea travellers. (If this seems confusing forget all modern concepts of boundaries.)

The discussions and findings of this Council give a more clear and concise picture

The Council of Trent

Trento

of the issues of the Protestant Reformation than almost any other single source. Transubstantiation, the necessary sacrificial ritual of the mass, seven sacraments, purgatory, indulgences,[60] celibate clergy: all these were upheld. Papal authority was enlarged, which Pius IV instantly employed to decide things not clearly settled at Trento.

The old scholastic verbiage of theological definitions, with curses for all disagreement, was renewed. The Bible and tradition were adjudged equal sources of truth—Rome's tradition, that is, and no one else's. Jerome's Latin Vulgate was declared the normative text. On every point Lutherans, Zwinglians and Calvinists were condemned, along with anything remotely resembling Anabaptism. There was no longer even a glimmer of reconciliation.

Rather, Rome with its newly reaffirmed self-confidence and its Jesuit special forces set out to conquer the world. Their techniques seemed to be led with all the issues that the Reformation was calling into question. Rome ensconced themselves in the mission field well before the eighteenth century Protestant missionary movement began. (Never forget, though, the quiet, ongoing work of the United Brethren and the Moravians. God will always have His workers.)

Concluding thoughts

It is distressing now to realise just what level of compromise there has since been on those very things identified at Trent (albeit negatively) as the core doctrines of the Protestant Reformation. Writing in 1963 as editor in the *Free Grace Record*, J. C. Doggett declared, 'The Editor grows increasingly certain that repentance and reformation are the great needs of all the Protestant Churches today'.[61]

Reformation, indeed, would be welcome in our day: reform not only of the world around us, but of the church itself. The Apostle Peter wrote in the first century,

'For the time *is come* that judgment must begin at the house of God: and if *it* first *begin* at us, what shall the end *be* of them that obey not the gospel of God?' (1 Peter 4.17). If this was true then, how much more true today! Yet in God's providence the Reformation started by Martin Luther five hundred years ago continues in our century, as God sovereignly brings about His will in the world.

And this brings us back to earlier thoughts.

Both Old and New Testaments show the Scriptures as an instrument of reform unto the people of God. Consider the finding of the Book of the Law in Josiah's day (2 Kings 22–23), and the words from the risen Christ and King to the seven churches of Revelation 2–3. Neither of those striking Bible summons to reform effected a once-for-all recovery amongst God's people. Nor did the Reformation, even though the first of the Ninety-five Theses reads, 'Our Lord and Master Jesus Christ in saying: "Repent ye", etc., intended that the whole life of believers should be penitence'. Luther had well understood the sense of the seven letters to the churches of Revelation as 'Remember, Repent, and Do!' Over so many zealous conflicts we should hear the voice of our Lord Jesus Christ declaring, 'Ye do err, not knowing the scriptures, nor the power of God' (Matthew 22.29).

59. The dukes of Austria were also the counts of Tyrol and dominated the region until 1918.

60. Though with strictures on their sale!

61. *Free Grace Record*, winter 1962–1963, vol. 3, no. 1, p. 5.

12: Appendices

An early Bible society

A Bible society is an organisation devoted to the translation, publication and distribution of the Christian Scriptures, usually at low cost to enable even those with limited means to have the Bible. Many believe that Bible societies are a recent—e.g. during the last couple of centuries—innovation, and think primarily of the British and Foreign Bible Society which began in 1804. However, we must go back another century to find their beginnings. The first fruit of this cause was the *Cansteinsche Bibelanstalt* founded in the early eighteenth century in Halle, Germany.

August Hermann Francke

In the latter years of the seventeenth century, August Hermann Francke was appointed pastor of the church in Glaucha, a town near Halle, Germany. While there he founded a school for poor children and an orphanage. In time his work grew to include a publishing house and printing office.

Baron Carl Hildebrand von Canstein was born at Lindenberg on 4 August 1667. He studied law at Frankfurt-on-the-Oder, and from 1686 to 1688 he toured the Netherlands, England, France, Italy and southern Germany, returning to Berlin. In Flanders during the Nine Years' War—which settled William of Orange on the English throne—he fell seriously ill. Returning to Berlin he devoted himself to philanthropy.

Canstein and Francke became friends in the late seventeenth century. With Philipp Spener they established the Canstein Bible Institute in hopes of producing inexpensive German Bibles by using the newly-in-use stereotype plate printing. They raised money from subscriptions and published a 2-groschen (about 4 cents) New Testament in 1712 and a 6-groschen (12 cents) full Bible in 1713.

In Canstein's lifetime they published about 100,000 New Testaments in twenty-eight editions, and some forty thousand full Bibles in octavo and duodecimo editions. There were Polish and Czech editions

Baron Carl Hildebrand von Canstein

printed in 1722, Wendish (spoken in Germany) and Lithuanian in 1868 and 1869. In 1892, the institute printed a first revised version of Luther's Bible. World War II interrupted work, but the modern Canstein Bible Institute was established in 1995, using the historic premises of the original institute.

Concordances

A concordance is an alphabetical list of words in the Bible, with indications of where they occur. The first concordance (other than any private compilations which surely existed) appeared in 1230. It was compiled by Hugo de Saint-Cher and his fellow Dominicans. Necessarily using the Latin Vulgate it had no 'verse references' as we now use. Stephen Langton, Archbishop of Canterbury between 1207 and 1228 (and accidental progenitor of Magna Carta), first divided the Bible into our now familiar arrangement of chapters. However, Hugo de Saint-Cher had his own system, dividing chapters into seven roughly equal sections, designated A to G. This can be seen in our early Tyndale New Testaments; however, it is Langton's chapter arrangement that is in use today across most languages—original and translation—and using verse divisions as introduced by Robert Stephens in 1545.

A first printed concordance appeared at Strasburg in 1470, with a second edition in 1475, and another at Nuremberg in 1485. These, with some unlikely lists of controversial passages, were the basis of the concordance published in 1555 by Robert Stephens. Stephens added proper names, supplied omissions, and placed all words in alphabetical order, with reference to all passages by verse as well as by chapter. The combined power of print and Reformation completed our basic Bible reference tool.

If you are now muttering eSword or BibleWorks and other such, these are only digitised presentations of the same data. I use them, but still make use of my paper copy of *Young's Concordance*, a dear gift from friends when I started Bible college many decades ago.

Commentaries

In Christian terms, a commentary is 'a study of a book (or of several books) of the Bible that employs linguistic, critical, historical, and theological disciplines and insights'.[62]

Comments on written material began with the scholia, handwritten marginal notes in classical works—subject to a great deal of change, quite personal and neither scholastic nor even useful in many cases. There could be no consistency across multiple copies. In the mercies of Providence printing coincided with the renewal of interest in the classical languages and their exegesis. The understanding of Scripture as the only basis of Christian doctrine led quickly to the realisation that the sense of the text was within Scripture alone, not behind it, under it or mystically beyond it; it was not a Gnostic secret nor reserved for church interpretation. This agrees well with the understanding that the Scripture was divinely appointed and inspired communication, and that the human authors were instruments of the Holy Spirit.

The Reformers generated significant and robust discussion of Biblical interpretation. This was to be seen in Luther's prefaces to all the books of the Bible and his *Open Letter on Translating*. Zwingli contributed *On the Clarity and Certainty of the Word*; and also came Bucer's short treatise on the method of reading Scripture in which he stressed studying the Gospels then moving on to the Pauline epistles as the core of Scripture, before the reading of the Old Testament. Heinrich Bullinger's *Decades* deal with fundamental themes of the Reformation, and particularly that the church does not date from the birth of Christ, nor from Pentecost, but with the promise of the woman's Seed in Genesis 3.15. So impressed was the English Archbishop Whitgift with the *Decades* that in 1568 he ordered that every clergyman should obtain a copy, and read at least one section every week.

Expounders and commentators of the Reformation era differed considerably in their

Luther at his desk in the Wartburg Castle

application of all this. Luther displayed a profound Trinitarian and Christological content throughout the Old Testament, especially in the Psalms. Peter Martyr Vermigli followed Luther's pattern, whilst Calvin was more restrained. Test issues included the creation testimony of Genesis 1, contending that three Persons are distinguished; Psalms—is every mention of David also of Christ? Emphasis on the text brought us commentaries rooted in Hebrew and Greek texts, increasingly available in well-edited printed editions. These provided good ground for continuing translations of text into vernacular languages and also into Latin, still the shared language of European education and scholarship. Protestant commitment to the text of Scripture and a theology based on it bore a rich harvest in Biblical exegetical commentary.

This harvest of commentaries covered every book of the Bible: a Biblical exegetical view of the whole of theology. The major commentators—Luther, Oecolampadius, Ulrich Zwingli, Konrad Pellikan, Martin Bucer and Calvin—show remarkable balance of interest in Old and New Testament. Luther, famous for his lectures on Romans and Galatians, was also a thoroughgoing Old Testament expositor, as seen in his works on Psalms, Genesis, Deuteronomy, Judges, Ecclesiastes, Isaiah and the Minor Prophets. Melanchthon wrote on Genesis, select Psalms, Proverbs, Daniel and Ecclesiastes as well as Colossians and John. John Calvin, though, was the outstanding Reformed commentator of the sixteenth century as he preached, lectured and commented through nearly the entire Bible.

62. F. B. Huey, Jr. and Bruce Corley, *A Student's Dictionary for Biblical and Theological Studies* (Grand Rapids, MI, USA: Zondervan Corp., 1983), p. 47.